Exquisite Embellishments for Your Clothes

Exquisite Embellishments
for Your Clothes

Valerie Van Arsdale Shrader

LARK BOOKS

A Division of Sterling Publishing Co., Inc.
New York

ART DIRECTOR: Susan McBride

PHOTOGRAPHER: Keith Wright

COVER DESIGNER: Barbara Zaretsky

ASSISTANT EDITOR: Rebecca Guthrie

ASSOCIATE ART DIRECTOR: Shannon Yokeley

ART INTERN: Bradley Norris

EDITORIAL INTERNS: David Squires
and Kelly J. Johnson

EDITORIAL ASSISTANCE: Delores Gosnell

Acknowledgments

Exquisite Embellishments for Your Clothes was based on a simple concept, that of taking a purchased garment and decorating it. But this little idea could not have blossomed into a beautiful book without the contributions of many talented people.

The team of art director Susan McBride and photographer Keith Wright made the book look irresistible. Models Loretta Ball, Candice Gillilard, and Rain Newcomb beautifully inhabited the embellished garments, and stylist Dana McCoy made the models look wonderful.

Ms. McBride made the photographs come to life in her inspired design, which perfectly expressed the personality of the projects.

My most sincere praise goes to the gifted designers, who understood the book instinctively and applied their creativity to deliver projects that truly captured the spirit of the book. Their biographies are on page 127; please take a moment to read about these inventive folks.

Asheville, North Carolina, is a vibrant little mountain city full of unique people and businesses. Many of the designers frequented the following shops and received helpful advice along the way, so I'd like to say thank you to these fine establishments: Fabric and Lace; Make Me!; House of Fabrics; and Waechter's Silk Shop. And lastly, thanks to the staff at Lark Books (especially Rebecca Guthrie, assistant editor) for technical assistance and moral support.

Library of Congress Cataloging-in-Publication Data

Shrader, Valerie Van Arsdale.
  Exquisite embellishments for your clothes / Valerie Van Arsdale Shrader.
     p. cm.
  Includes index.
  ISBN 1-57990-684-2
  1. Fancy work. 2. Clothing and dress. I. Title.
TT750.S58 2006
646.4'04--dc22

                                        2005016775

10 9 8 7 6 5 4 3 2 1

First Edition

Published by Lark Books, A Division of
Sterling Publishing Co., Inc.
387 Park Avenue South, New York, N.Y. 10016

© 2006, Lark Books

Distributed in Canada by Sterling Publishing,
c/o Canadian Manda Group, 165 Dufferin Street
Toronto, Ontario, Canada M6K 3H6

Distributed in the U.K. by Guild of Master Craftsman Publications Ltd.,
Castle Place, 166 High Street, Lewes, East Sussex, England BN7 1XU
Tel: (+ 44) 1273 477374, Fax: (+ 44) 1273 478606, e-mail: pubs@thegmcgroup.com,
Web: www.gmcpublications.com

Distributed in Australia by Capricorn Link (Australia) Pty Ltd.,
P.O. Box 704, Windsor, NSW 2756 Australia

If you have questions or comments about this book,
please contact:
Lark Books
67 Broadway
Asheville, NC 28801
(828) 253-0467

Manufactured in China

ISBN 13: 978-1-57990-684-9
ISBN 10: 1-57990-684-2

For information about custom editions, special sales, premium and corporate purchases, please contact Sterling Special Sales Department at 800-805-5489 or specialsales@sterlingpub.com.

Contents

Introduction

* Express your personality through your embellished clothes. Look for the sweater project on page 66 and the skirt on page 88.

* A crocheted flower, a silk bloom, a fabric posy, or fanciful pins can all be used to embellish items in your wardrobe.

S hopping for a special occasion is *so* much fun. When you're invited to a party and have a look in mind, isn't it a great adventure to prowl your favorite shops to find the perfect little dress? At the first boutique, you find something that's almost right, but the skirt is too long. Later on in the morning, you see one that's close: Oh, you think, if only this dress had a little sparkle, it would be perfect! Perhaps you'll find a charming frock, but you dare not even look at the price because you know it's just too expensive to even dream about buying. Yes, shopping is fun—but it's sometimes frustrating, too.

Fortunately, there's a creative solution to the shopping dilemma. Enhance your sense of style by personally embellishing your wardrobe. Women have always understood the need to create a style—an aura, if you will—and *Exquisite Embellishments for Your Clothes* will guide you along that path. Decorating your clothes is both an expression of your personality *and* a creative outlet. Presented here are more than 50 ways to take a purchased garment or accessory and use it as a blank canvas. Look at a simple sheath and imagine it enlivened with a handmade scarf with velvet accents. Think of a plain linen blouse blooming with colorful decorative stitching and elegant pintucks. A pair of sleek black mules becomes your footwear staple for an entire season by quickly accessorizing them with jewelry.

✳ Add special touches like lace insets, ribbon trim, and decorative stitching to a plain linen skirt.

Jewelry can be a quick and easy way to personalize your garments or accessories.

In addition to dozens of imaginative projects, there are several examples of ways to embellish the same item with different techniques to demonstrate the options at your disposal. Some of the projects can be created with the most basic of techniques, yet there are garments to inspire the experienced seamstress, too.

When you see haute couture on the runway, with sumptuously beaded garments or yards of embroidered silk, did you know that the designers generally rely on professionals to create these lavish embellishments? Specialty firms are often contracted to create the spectacular details that make a particular article of clothing so captivating. In a real sense, you can become this specialty embellisher when you adorn your clothing. Just as important, you'll learn how to get the look and feel of an expensive garment for much less than what you might pay if you purchased a similar item from a chic catalog or an exclusive boutique. Specific instruction is given on every type of embellishment used, including techniques such as embroidery and appliqué.

These techniques can be used to decorate something from your existing wardrobe, a vintage find from a thrift store, or a new garment purchased at an end-of-season sale. All it takes is a keen eye and a little imagination. Now, shopping becomes nothing *but* fun when you look for a simple garment to decorate in your own distinctive way. Appliqué or embroider, add beads or ribbons, even deconstruct a garment to make it something truly your own. Create a lasting impression when you express your style by embellishing your clothing.

Expressing Your Style

T he key to embellishing your clothing is recognizing the potential in each garment and using your skills to create your own signature look. Do you love embroidery? Luxe treatments such as couched metallic threads and sequins? Maybe your taste runs more to ruffles and lace, tulle accents, or silk appliqués. Whatever your style, you may be surprised at how quickly you can create a wardrobe that expresses your personality. By starting with a purchased item, you've already got the fit and color you want. And by using your talents—or learning a few skills—you can customize your clothes to make a unique statement.

Choosing a Garment to Embellish

When your favorite catalog comes to your mailbox, and you marvel over the wondrous things within, think about how you can capture the essence of a piece you love as well as create a project that expresses your own inimitable sense of style. Pretend you're looking over my shoulder while I browse through an actual catalog to search for possibilities.

Look at the charming cover. It features a linen skirt with a series of dainty ruffles at the hem, each ruffle constructed of a different fabric. Create this mood by adding your own multi-fabric ruffles to an existing skirt, as shown above. Let's flip through the catalog a few more pages, where we'll find a smart canvas jacket accented by a silk rosette pin. Our chic wool jacket, shown at the top right on page 9, was a thrift-store find that needed only a little velvet and a few pearls to become fabulous. Finally, a couple of pages later, there's a charming long-sleeved tee with hand-crocheted appliqués. Get this look by using a simple macramé technique to add silk ribbon cuffs, as you'll see at the top left on page 9.

Within the first 10 pages of this lovely catalog, we've already identified three ways to translate inspiration into a personal expression of style. Take the same focus with you to the mall, your favorite thrift shops, or your own closet to look for potential projects. And remember that you're making a statement about your own style and what appeals to you; the garments you find don't need to be exceptionally trendy to be perfect for the kinds of projects you'll see in *Exquisite Embellishments for Your Clothes*.

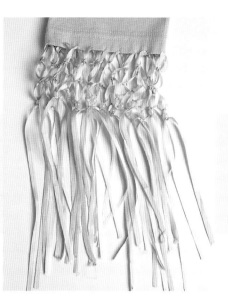

These embellished garments capture the feel of actual offerings in a catalogue, and all were inexpensively purchased and easily decorated.

Garment Characteristics

There are some important considerations to bear in mind when you're planning an embellishment project; because you're working with a garment that has already been constructed, you must think about how easily your decorative technique can be executed within the garment's original design. To help determine an item's potential, here are some characteristics to keep in mind.

Access

Since most embellishment techniques require ready access to both the right and the wrong sides of a garment, construction is a major consideration. Garments made from woven material that feature simple lines are good candidates for embellishing. For instance, an A-line skirt can be easily decorated in a number of ways, either by handwork or by sewing machine. It can be embroidered, beaded, appliquéd, or festooned with ribbons or trim of all varieties. A blouse that buttons down the front is also a good candidate, as you can easily access the front and back.

Pants can be quite successfully embellished, but they do pose some accessibility issues if you plan to decorate the legs; bear in mind that you'll probably have to rip out the seams to adorn them with ease.

Shoes can be a little tricky because there's not much room to work inside, so consider shoes such as the mules you see on page 30 that have easily accessible surfaces. In general, fabric shoes are easier to decorate than leather ones.

※ A basic skirt is a good choice for embellishment because it's easy to access and has no conflicting construction details.

✳ This blouse was altered significantly during the embellishment process; many possibilities are available to you if your sewing skills are strong. The original blouse is above, with the altered blouse below.

Details

If you're considering a garment that already has embellishment details such as pleats or ruching, be sure to think about how these elements will be affected by your decoration. For example, an appliqué won't lie flat near gathers; if you stitch over a pleat, you lose the movement this detail creates. A flat canvas such as an A-line skirt, a sheath, or a simple buttoned blouse allows your embellishment to be more noticeable and simpler to execute.

Unless you want to deconstruct a garment completely to add details within its structure, such as a row of pleating across the back of a blouse, you'll want to work within the confines of the garment's original construction. If your sewing skills are strong, however, the opportunities to deconstruct a garment are almost endless. For example, the blouse shown at the left was altered by removing the original sleeves, adding tucks, and creating a decorative hem.

Fabric Type

Knit garments pose some challenges because you must be conscious of retaining the stretch of the piece when you apply any technique. For example, applying trim with a straight stitch negates the stretch in the garment. Zigzag stitching helps maintain some stretch in this circumstance.

Many of the projects that are featured in the section that begins on page 24 include photographs of the garments before they were embellished, so it may be helpful to peruse this section to see what types of ready-made clothing and accessories are easily and successfully embellished.

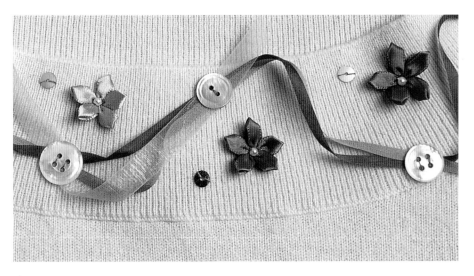

✳ Consider the laundering requirements of both your original garment and the embellishments you add. The collage along the neckline of this cashmere sweater can be easily removed and quickly replaced after dry cleaning.

Care of Embellished Garments

Before you even contemplate embellishing a garment or an accessory, consider how you'll launder the item. In most cases, dry cleaning or gentle hand washing will be required. Begin with the instructions listed on the purchased garment's label. Then, if you think you'll be able to hand wash your garment after embellishing it, test all the materials you use (including beads) for colorfastness. Another approach is to plan your project so the embellishments can be removed easily for cleaning. (Temporary embellishments offer you an opportunity to create a new decoration after washing, so this is a versatile approach.) Don't neglect to consider this very important detail.

Choosing an Embellishment Technique

✳ Feel free to use several different decorative techniques on the same garment. This dress features simple bead embroidery and the addition of velvet ribbon ties.

L ooking closely at our catalog again, you may notice that the simple pintucks used in a linen blouse add charm and sophistication. *Simple* is the key word, because embellishment need not be lavish to be beautiful. Easy embroidery, decorative machine stitching, and basic appliqué can all be applied successfully. Many of the lovely projects in this book use several techniques in the same project, so remember to think in terms of combining various embellishment styles. The following section discusses the basic techniques of many types of embellishment; perhaps you'll be inspired to add a new skill to your repertoire.

Techniques

A general knowledge of sewing and handwork will allow you to employ many creative techniques to decorate your clothes. Here's an overview of the methods used in this book; the projects section that is the heart of the book begins on page 24. That section will provide more specific instructions in the context of a particular garment, and the Illustrated Techniques & Glossary on page 120 offers additional help with many of the ideas suggested below.

Decorative Stitching

At the most basic level, you can use the stitches on your machine as devices to enhance purchased clothing. Since even basic machines often offer some decorative stitches, you can use these when you're stitching on ribbon or appliqués for added appeal. Try making a contrasting thread an additional visual element. Both of the ideas discussed above are illustrated in the photo on page 13. A simple zigzag stitch in a contrasting thread is a clever effect, too.

✳ A decorative stitch done in contrasting thread is an easy embellishment technique.

Ruffles

A *ruffle* is simply a strip of fabric that is gathered to fit your garment. It can be easily added to a neckline, a hem, or a cuff. If you want a ruffle with gentle drape, make it from a soft fabric; if you want a ruffle with more body, use a stiffer fabric.

A single ruffle is gathered along one long edge and added to an area such as a hem or is sewn into a seam. A double ruffle is gathered between its two long edges and sewn onto the surface of a garment (you may also see a double ruffle referred to as a *ruche*).

To make a simple ruffle, finish one edge and add two rows of long stitching to the other edge. Keep the thread ends long and simply pull to gather the ruffle to the approximate length needed. Pin in place and adjust the gathers for balance.

Tucks

Tucks are stitched folds that can be used as a delightful decorative element. You can shorten a skirt or pair of pants by making a series of tucks along the hem, for instance. To form a simple tuck on the outside of the fabric, fold the fabric wrong sides together and stitch to the desired width along the folded edge; repeat for each tuck. *Pintucks*, which are very narrow tucks, can be created either manually as described above or with the use of a special pintucking presser foot, an accessory for your sewing machine.

If you're adding tucks to a purchased item, remember to look for a garment that has excess length or width so there is enough fabric to allow for the creation of the tucks.

This skirt was infused with color by using a variegated scarf to make piping and a decorative hem. The remnants of the scarf were sewn in place at the waist.

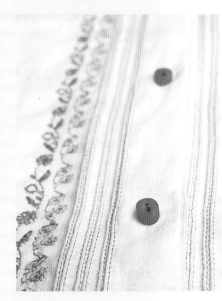

A linen blouse is enlivened with machine embroidery and pintucks. New buttons were added to complete the transformation.

Deconstruction and Altering

Scissors and a seam ripper are important and powerful tools. You can slash a skirt to add piping and a decorative edging, as shown at the left, or remove seams to allow easier access to an article of clothing.

You can also change the shape of a hemline, a cuff, or a collar, giving a garment an entirely new personality, as you'll see in several of the projects. Some dressmaking experience will be helpful when planning extensive altering of a garment.

Embroidery

Embroidery is a classic form of embellishment, refined throughout the centuries. Beautiful accents can be added with simple hand stitches, as you'll see in several projects in this book. Refer to the Illustrated Techniques & Glossary on page 124 for information on the embroidery stitches used in this book.

If your sewing machine offers embroidery stitches, you have a realm of possibilities for decorating clothing. You may need some additional accessories for your machine, such as a special presser foot or needle, so check your manual to see which items you may need. If you don't own a machine that offers embroidery stitches, you can also use rows of simple stitches as a substitute—lines of topstitching or zigzag stitching

done with variegated thread, for example. The clever use of the stitches available to you can emulate the look of true machine embroidery.

Crewel

Crewel is a specific form of embroidery in which wool thread is used. Crewel wool, though often used for tapestry work, can also be used for embroidery, as you see on page 15.

Appliqué

Appliqué is the applying of one fabric layer to another. This technique is more varied than it may seem, because you can combine embellishment methods to outline an appliqué with decorative stitching, for example, or further embellish an appliqué with sequins or beads.

You can create your own appliqué designs, cutting the fabric to the shape desired. Apply appliqués to the garment in any number of ways—with paper-backed fusible web, with hand stitching, or with decorative machine stitching such as satin stitch. Finish the edges for a polished look, or leave the edges raw for an unconstructed feel. Of course, you can use purchased appliqués to enliven a garment or an accessory. Great vintage appliqué pieces are available in addition to contemporary items.

Weaving

You may not have considered weaving as an embellishment method, but it can be a remarkably easy technique. A sweater with large knit stitches offers the perfect opportunity to simply weave ribbons in and out using a yarn needle. A straw hat or a pair of strappy sandals may also lend themselves well to weaving. You can also create an area for weaving by making buttonholes in fabric. A body-conscious knit top would be a good candidate for this technique, for example.

Beading

Elaborate bead embroidery, while luxurious and dazzling, is time-consuming and requires a certain level of experience to achieve successful results. However, you can add *joie de vivre* to purchased garments or accessories with some simple beading accents. Read more about basic bead embroidery on page 122.

Crochet

Several simple crochet stitches have been used in this book. With a simple hook and some yarn, you can create a memorable edging for a garment or an accessory; see the capelet on page 86 for a fine example. For more information about the easy stitches used here, see page 121 in the the Illustrated Techniques & Glossary.

Macramé

Simple square knots can create a surprisingly sophisticated decoration, especially if they're made from luxurious silk ribbon. A contemporary interpretation of *macramé* can include the use of novelty yarns.

Felting

Several projects in this book make use of *felted* wool. Wool is all too easily felted in hot water in the washing machine, as you may know from past mishaps. The heat and agitation of the washer causes the fibers to meld together, and when rinsed in cool water the wool forms a dense mat. The resulting felted wool isn't prone to raveling and can be incorporated in any number of ways. Felting is quite easy. Start with an item that's at least 50 percent wool (the more wool, the better, as synthetic fibers alone will not felt). Toss it in the washing machine with warm water. Check on the item every now and then; when it's felted to your satisfaction, rinse in cool water. If you want the item to felt thoroughly, dry it in the dryer; otherwise, let it air dry.

Crewelwork motifs add flair to a pair of jeans.

Woven ribbons are a wonderfully effortless adornment for a sweater.

Quick & Easy Embellishment

There are several easy ways to adorn your wardrobe without fuss. Costume jewelry offers many possibilities and can be switched out quickly to suit your mood. Clip-on earrings can be added to shoes in a flash, and a grouping of brooches brightens a hat or a waistline.

Another delightfully simple idea is to switch out the plain buttons on your garment for more decorative ones, adding instant color and visual interest. On this hat, buttons and basic stitches transform a mere hat into a fashion statement.

Choosing an Embellishment Material

After you choose a technique, there are still other decisions to be made, for the embellishments themselves are the key to expressing your style. If you want to add trim, will it be rickrack or *passementerie*? If you're embroidering, will you use cotton floss or opulent silk thread? Will you add silk appliqués or cotton ruffles? Shopping for just the right accoutrements is the most enjoyable part of the entire process of embellishing your wardrobe. Plan to spend an unhurried afternoon combing your favorite shops.

✳Experiment with different materials to properly express your sense of style.

When you shop for materials, be sure to bring your garment or accessory with you to coordinate color and texture. And be sure to purchase enough ribbon, lace, or buttons to complete your project. Of course, it's entirely possible that you already have a fine collection of embellishments and you're approaching this process from the opposite perspective by looking for clothes to add embellishments *to*. Whatever your approach, remember to enjoy the search.

Sewing Notions

Many familiar items in your sewing basket can also serve as an embellishment. Read about some of them below.

Thread

Although thread is an important functional item, it can be decorative as well. Specialty threads offer a quick, easy, and inexpensive embellishment, and metallic or variegated threads add sophistication when used for topstitching or machine embroidery.

Seam Tape or Binding

Normally used to cover and finish raw edges, these notions can also be used like trim; particularly beautiful is the lustrous rayon seam binding used in tailoring. You can also make your own continuous bias strips from fabric to create binding that is truly your own.

Buttons

In addition to serving a utilitarian function, decorative buttons can add flair to a garment that needs a little something extra. From gleaming mother-of-pearl to funky glass buttons and everything in between, buttons are available in every style and size.

Decorative Trims

Ribbon, lace, rickrack, or piping? Any of these trims are versatile additions to a purchased garment. Used alone or in combination, decorative trim offers immediate impact for your clothes.

Ribbon

Nothing is more unabashedly feminine than ribbon, and it's a multipurpose embellishment. It can be used as striking appliqué or as a closure. Ribbon is available in plush velvet, wispy organza, and textured *grosgrain*, to name just a few, and specialty ribbon that's pleated or ruched is also available. You can mix and match widths and textures for visual excitement.

Lace

For a decidedly romantic feel, add a lace inset or a ruffled lace hem. You can find lace in varying widths (with stretch or without), and although some laces can be quite expensive, just a yard or two can be a beautiful addition to a simple garment.

Rickrack

If you're feeling playful, add some colorful rickrack. Rickrack is available in a variety of widths and in specialty finishes and weaves; you can also find metallic or variegated styles.

Piping

Piping is inserted into a seam, so if you're interested in deconstructing garments, you can add piping to accent a seamline or create a colorful contrast.

Braid

Specialty braids such as soutache and middy have differing textures—soutache is woven in a herringbone pattern, for instance—and can be found in various colors and widths. *Passementerie* is a sophisticated technique involving the use of braid and/or other trim worked in intricate patterns.

Beaded Trim

If you lack the time or expertise to do complicated beading, consider adding a beaded trim to a garment. With simple whipstitching, you can add glamour to an uninspiring garment. From a narrow string of faux pearls to a wide band of decorated lace, beads define luxury.

Custom Trim

It's remarkably simple to create your own unique trim—it's as easy as layering ribbon and stitching them together with a decorative stitch, as shown at the right. Use different types of trim together for an intriguing result. Stitch on beads or sequins to mimic the look of expensive couture trim.

With just a pair of pinking shears, you can fashion faux rickrack from felt. Or you can use a bias tape maker to create trim from fabric. There are lots of opportunities for creativity when partnering trims and decorative elements, such as those discussed in the section on the following page.

✳ Felt "rickrack" is simply cut with a pair of pinking shears.

✳ Here are some samples of handmade trim created with decorative stitching.

19

✳ Embroidery floss can add a bit of color and pattern to a plain garment.

✳ Embellishment should be fun! This skirt features a felted appliqué decorated with embroidery and tiny buttons.

Decorative Elements

Individual baubles such as beads or sequins can add personality to your wardrobe. Likewise, the choice of fabric for an appliqué or just the right floss for an embroidered neckline can make all the difference in your final product.

Sequins

Lightweight and inexpensive sequins can add simple sparkle or dazzling emphasis. Sequins come in many shapes and finishes (shiny as well as matte) and can be applied using several different techniques. *Paillettes* are larger than sequins and have holes not in the center but at the edge.

✳ Simple bead embroidery is quick to learn.

Beads

These little gems can be lavishly applied or used as a simple accent. Delicate seed beads can be affixed with simple running stitches, or you may choose to add a few chunky beads for emphasis. The basic techniques are simple to learn, as you will see on page 122. Remember to check beads for colorfastness *before* you launder.

Eyelets and Grommets

The addition of a series of eyelets or grommets can allow you to weave ribbon or trim as you see in the pants on page 106; they're easily applied with an eyelet setter or grommet-setting tool.

Fabric

Don't overlook fabric as a decorative element. The use of fabric appliqués is a charming way to add dimension, color, and pattern to your garments all at the same time. Experiment with the use of different fabrics and appliqué styles; add other embellishments such as buttons, beads, or sequins to make an appliqué a work of art.

You can also add ruffles of contrasting fabric. As pertains to any embellishment technique, keep the laundering requirements in mind if you add fabric to an existing garment; if you sew silk to a cotton garment, for example, you will likely have to hand wash or dry-clean it when laundering is required. To compare fabric possibilities, see the skirt with silk appliqués on page 114 and the skirt with ruffles on page 70.

Embroidery Threads

Cotton, silk, rayon, and linen threads each offer different luster and texture; metallic threads offer irresistible sheen. Use whichever appeals to your taste and don't hesitate to combine the types, either. Silk ribbon embroidery is also beautiful but has some specialized techniques that pertain to that medium. Wool floss is used in crewelwork, as seen on the jeans on page 100. Specialized threads are also available if you're interested in machine embroidery.

✳ Basic sewing supplies will often be used while working on a project.

Tools

With just a few tools, you can create the special decorations that express your matchless style. Here's a review of the kinds of tools that aid in successful embellishing. Each set of project instructions will have information about the specific tools and materials used to create it.

Needles and Pins

Have a variety of needles for handwork; an assortment that includes embroidery, chenille, yarn, and beading needles should suffice for many techniques. Embroidery needles are sharp, with large eyes; chenille needles are somewhat thicker, for use with heavy threads; yarn (or tapestry) needles are blunt and were used for the weaving projects in this book. Long, thin beading needles are perfect for working with tiny seed beads.

Dressmaker's pins are suitable for general use, but you may want to have some thin silk pins on hand for delicate projects.

Sewing Machine

While there are many projects in this book that don't require a sewing machine, it will certainly offer you more options. It need not be an expensive computerized machine to give you excellent results with hemming, making your own trim, altering a sleeve, or using decorative stitches.

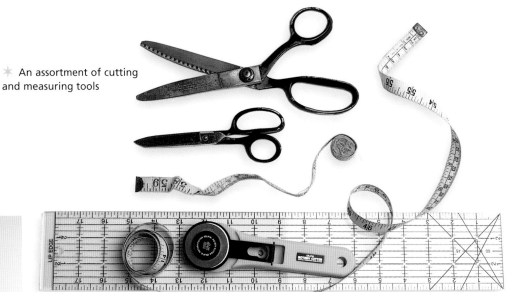

✳ An assortment of cutting and measuring tools

✳ Fusible web was perfect for the inventive appliqué technique used on these pants.

Fortunately, even the most basic machines now offer at least a few specialty stitches.

Cutting Tools

Good, well-sharpened scissors will speed your work considerably and make it free of stress. A pair of dressmaker's shears (straight or bent handle) and a pair of pinking shears are good tools to have on hand.

A rotary cutter can also be a great help in cutting strips of fabric, as for bias strips or ruffles. Used in conjunction with a cutting mat and a quilter's ruler, the rotary cutter makes for quick and accurate cutting.

A seam ripper is the seamstress's best friend. Use it to rip out existing seams if you're deconstructing a garment and, of course, to correct mistakes.

Measuring Tools

Keep a tape measure and a sewing gauge on hand. A see-through quilter's ruler, mentioned above, is handy for measuring and cutting. Accurate measuring will help insure the success of your embellishment project.

Marking Tools

Oftentimes you'll need to mark the placement of trim or other embellishments. You can use tailor's chalk, dressmaker's pencils, or water-soluble or vanishing ink markers. Make sure you test any of the above in an inconspicuous place to be certain the markings can be removed or will disappear as advertised.

Another item you may find useful is quilter's tape. It's a valuable tool to mark lines for placement purposes.

Fusible and Stabilizer Products

There are a number of products that can make your embellishing work much easier. Fusible products, such as a roll of bonding web or sheets of paper-backed fusible web, can reduce or eliminate sewing or basting, offering a no-sew alternative for techniques like appliqué. Some fusible products offer advantages, including the ability to bond temporarily, so investigate the various types to find the ones that best suit your purpose.

Liquid seam sealant helps prevent fraying of raw edges and can be helpful when you perhaps don't want the extra thickness of a folded edge in a narrow hem. Tear-away or water-soluble stabilizers are needed for machine embroidery or sewing with delicate fabrics. Stabilizers do exactly what their name implies: they add a supporting layer that helps provide proper tension and prevents bunching, puckering, or stretching while you work.

Pressing Tools

As with dressmaking, you will no doubt need to use an iron with some embellishment techniques. A good steam iron and a sturdy ironing board are required tools, but it's important that you test any trims to make sure they can withstand the heat of the iron. A pressing cloth may be necessary for certain items you use for decoration.

✳ **Choose the projects that express your personality.**

Using This Book

Let the projects in this book spark your imagination. Look through the projects section that begins on the next page to explore the possibilities—see what types of garments or accessories lend themselves to embellishing. Likewise, the types of embellishments used will let you know what's within the range of your abilities and interests; be warned that some are so enticing that you may want to learn a new skill. If you're interested in exploring a new technique, browse through the Illustrated Techniques & Glossary section on page 120 for an overview.

On a practical note, bear in mind that your actual project will, in all likelihood, be a different size or a slightly different style than the garments used here. Approximate measurements have been given for all materials used; be sure to measure your actual garment before you buy any materials. Remember that the project instructions will include a detailed list of all the items that you need to create your own embellished skirt, blouse, scarf, or what have you. The materials are listed first, followed by the tools, so it will be easy to create a shopping list when you're ready to get started.

You'll be pleasantly surprised to learn how easy it is to customize purchased garments to express your creativity and reflect your personal style. Consider this a party invitation—the party we talked about at the beginning of the book. Now, go create something fabulous to wear!

Ribbon-Trimmed Surplice Top

A specialty ribbon and a trim with a hint of sparkle change this top from ordinary to extraordinary. The gathered ribbon complements the ruching in the garment.

Embellished by Valerie Shrader

Materials & Tools

Cotton/spandex surplice top

2-inch-wide gathered ribbon, approximately 1¼ yards

¼-inch-wide decorative trim, approximately 1¼ yards

Thread to match the decorative trim

Tape measure

Scissors

Dressmaker's pins

Sewing machine

Instructions

1 Measure and cut both the ribbon and the trim to the size of the surplice neckline, allowing an extra ½ inch to turn under the raw edges.

2 Pin the gathered ribbon to the wrong side of the neckline. Turn under the raw ends of the ribbon and baste in place following the seamline of the existing narrow hem. Use a long, narrow zigzag stitch to preserve as much of the stretch in the garment as possible.

3 Place the trim along the basting line on the right side of the garment, being sure to cover the stitching. Turn under the raw ends of the trim. Use thread in a matching color to stitch the narrow trim in place, again using a long, narrow zigzag stitch.

Blooming Blazer

Ribbon flowers with pearl button centers add panache
to this blazer, a special thrift-store find.

Embellished by Marthe Le Van

Materials & Tools

Wool blazer

1-inch-wide velvet ribbon, two different colors, approximately 2 to 3 yards each

Thread to match each ribbon

4 pearl buttons, each approximately ½ inch wide

Needle

Scissors

Dressmaker's pins

Instructions

1 Begin with one color of ribbon and its matching thread. Thread the needle and knot. Beginning under one corner of the ribbon, insert the needle through the ribbon from the wrong side, but do not pull the thread through.

2 Determine the size of your flower petals, and make a fold in the ribbon accordingly. Insert the needle into the first fold, but do not pull the thread through.

3 Continue to make folds in the ribbon and feed them onto the needle until the needle is full. At this point, pull the needle through and push the ribbon folds down the length of thread, flush against the knot.

4 Repeat the process of making folds, stacking them on the needle, and guiding them down the thread as shown below. (For clarity, contrasting thread is used in this example.) Continue until the natural curve of the gathered ribbon makes a complete circle.

5 Neatly turn under the ends of the ribbon where they meet, and sew them together. Cut off any excess ribbon.

6 Form as many simple ribbon flowers in as many colors as you wish (or until you run out of ribbon!). Arrange the flowers on your blazer to create a satisfying composition. Mark the location of each flower on the blazer by placing a straight pin through each flower's center.

7 Sew one pearl button onto the jacket at each pin. Slip one flower over each button. There's no need to sew the flowers onto the jacket, because the tension from the button will hold them in place.

8 If your jacket has pockets, accent them with a length of ribbon. Pin in place and stitch.

✳ Variation

Any type of round, domed button can be used for these ribbon flowers.

Pleated Silk Skirt

A sumptuous band of layered ribbon now defines this luxurious silk skirt. The topstitching on the yoke adds a subtle shine.

Embellished by Valerie Shrader

Materials & Tools

Silk skirt

⅞-inch-wide grosgrain ribbon, approximately 1 yard long

¼-inch-wide decorative ribbon, approximately 1 yard long

Roll of fusible bonding web (optional)

Metallic thread to match the decorative ribbon

Tape measure

Scissors

Sewing machine

Iron (optional)

Silk pins

✳ Variation

Add a bijou for extra sparkle.

Instructions

1 Measure and then cut both the grosgrain ribbon and the decorative ribbon to the circumference of the skirt's yoke, adding an extra ½ inch to turn under the raw edges.

2 Create your own trim by combining the wide grosgrain and the narrow decorative ribbons, stitching the latter on top of the former with a wide zigzag stitch. Experiment with small lengths of the ribbon until you set the proper stitch width; the stitch should extend across the width of the narrow decorative ribbon (see photo above). Jot down the setting to use in step 4.

3 If desired, use bonding web to turn under the edges of the ribbon. Alternatively, just press under the raw edges and stitch them in place when you sew the ribbons onto the skirt in steps 4 and 5.

4 Beginning at the zipper, pin and baste the grosgrain ribbon onto the skirt, placing the center of the ribbon on the yoke's seamline.

5 Use the line of basted stitches on the grosgrain ribbon for placement and stitch the narrow decorative ribbon on top using metallic thread; set your machine to the zigzag stitch that you determined in step 2.

6 For the pièce de résistance, use the metallic thread to outline some of the graphic elements in the fabric's design.

Variations on a Theme: Shoes

These sleek fabric mules are easily decorated in a variety of ways. A simple pair that you can embellish in many ways will be a versatile addition to your wardrobe.

Jewelry

Costume jewelry is a clever way to immediately customize your mules. Here are some ideas: two feature simple clip-on earrings, and the third gets its sparkle from a pair of identical brooches, pinned to the shoes in reverse orientation.

Dupioni Appliqués

Elegant silk dupioni squares can be coordinated with your ensemble. You'll need the following: two different colors of silk, about ¼ yard each; metallic thread; clear nylon thread; a needle; two sequins; and two pinwheels (these came from a vintage fabric shop). Cut two 3½-inch squares from each silk; ravel the edges. Place one square atop the other in a less-than-perfect alignment, so the bottom square peeks out below the top square. (To preserve the alignment, baste the two squares together, if desired, as shown below.) Stitch the pinwheel to one corner using the clear nylon thread. Add the sequin with the metallic thread, knotting on the outside. Fold the squares in half (more or less) and slide them onto the shoes, adjusting the placement as desired. Unfold the top half of the square before stitching it in place along the edge of the shoe, sewing through the half of the square that remains inside the shoe. Fold the top half of the square back over the front to finish. For a permanent attachment to the shoe, apply fabric glue to the inside of the shoe and slide the square over the shoe, bonding the bottom half of the square to the shoe. Press into place and let dry.

Fabric Roses

Add interesting dimension with these fabric roses; a thimble will be helpful as you stitch them on using clear nylon thread. Instead of trying to reach inside the shoe to begin stitching from the wrong side, you'll find it much easier to bury the knot inconspicuously on the right side of the shoe and stitch downward. For instance, these knots are buried between the leaves and the flowers, as are the stitches themselves. Sew in place using as few stitches as possible.

Sleeveless Top with Rickrack

When you're ready for some fun, indulge in a little rickrack.
Combine colors and widths for a playful expression of style.

Embellished by Valerie Shrader

Materials & Tools

Cotton sleeveless top

3 types of rickrack, in varying widths and colors, at least 1½ yards each

Thread to match each color of rickrack

Liquid seam sealant (optional)

Tape measure

Scissors

Dressmaker's pins

Sewing machine

Instructions

1 Measure the neckline around the front of the top and cut the narrowest rickrack to fit, adding an extra ½ inch or so. Measure around one side of the neckline and down the center front of the tank, adding a couple of extra inches. Cut two pieces from each of the remaining types of rickrack to this measurement.

2 Pin the narrow rickrack around the neckline as seen in the photo on page 32, beginning at one shoulder seam. Use a matching color of thread to stitch the rickrack to the tank.

3 Pin the widest rickrack next to the rickrack you sewed on in step 2; near the center of the top, pivot the rickrack to flow down the front of the top. Stitch in place using matching thread, ending the line of stitching 3 or 4 inches above the hem. Let the end of the rickrack streamer hang freely.

4 Repeat step 3 to add the remaining rickrack, but end the line of stitching midway down the front of the top.

5 If you prefer, apply liquid seam sealant to the raw edges of the rickrack.

Beaded Trim Tank Top

Spring and summer demand an endless assortment of tank tops and camisoles.
Take advantage of their fabulous colors and designs by embellishing the necklines with
your favorite trim, be it faux pearls or daisy chains.

Embellished by Stacey Budge

Materials & Tools

Cotton knit tank top

⅜-inch-wide beaded trim, approximately 1 yard

Thread to match the trim

Scissors

Dressmaker's pins

Needle

Instructions

1 Measure the neckline of the tank top and cut the beaded trim to the appropriate length, allowing a ¼-inch overlap.

2 Pin the trim along the edge of the neckline.

3 Using a whipstitch, sew the trim securely, overlapping the ends.

✳ Variation

Add frilly floral trim to a cotton/spandex camisole in much the same manner as described above, but with one major difference. Stitch the trim to the front and back neckline by hand or machine, *but do not stitch it to the straps in the same manner.* To preserve the stretch in the straps, tack the trim to the straps at several points rather than using a continuous line of stitching.

Dress with Bows

This delightfully simple idea can be used to highlight any circular motif.
These ribbon bows add a playful element to any garment or accessory.

Embellished by Valerie Shrader

Materials & Tools

Cotton dress with bold print

⅜-inch-wide grosgrain ribbon, at least two colors that complement the dress, each several yards long

Thread to match the dress

Buttons, at least two colors that complement the dress, each approximately ⅜ inch wide

Needle

Instructions

1 Make bows from the ribbon and tack together with a stitch or two. Then, stitch them onto the dress as desired; the bows on this dress were placed on top of the flowers in a random fashion.

2 Stitch the buttons onto the bows to disguise the stitching.

✳ Variation

If you want more translucent bows, use delicate organza ribbon rather than grosgrain.

Variations on a Theme: Hats

Hats offer a wonderful canvas to embellish, and sometimes the simplest concept yields the greatest success. Here are four ideas for inspiration.

Bejeweled Bucket Hat

A piece of costume jewelry adds easy, no-sew excitement to a basic hat. All you need is a large brooch. If your hat has a bow, like this one did, either remove it or fold it in on itself to tuck behind the brooch. Carefully pin the brooch to the hat.

Brown Cloche

This lovely brown hat already had some interesting tucks. But some colorful buttons and simple stitching make it much more interesting. You'll need the following tools and supplies: approximately 20 small buttons in varying colors, embroidery floss to match the colors of the buttons, and an embroidery needle. Use only one strand of contrasting floss to stitch on the buttons, adding a decorative stitch between each button. (See page 124 for embroidery stitches.) Knot the ends of the floss on the right side of the hat and leave them exposed. Continue adding rows of buttons as desired, using different stitches between the rows and varying the number of buttons in each row.

Appliquéd Bucket Hat

This lighthearted but elegant angora hat had rows of stitching around the brim that are now accented with faux felt rickrack. The flower appliqués have a twinkling sequin center. Use your sewing machine for this project, as well as these items: wool/rayon felt in three colors, ¼ yard of each color; a tape measure; scissors (both dressmaker's shears and pinking shears); thread to match the lightest color of felt; and two sequins. Measure around the brim and cut three strips of felt to that measurement. Use the pinking shears to create the rickrack effect, cutting each strip about ⅜ inch wide. Cut the remaining pieces of the appliqué using the dressmaker's shears. (Instead of applying the light green centers on top of the flowers, they were inlaid into a hole cut in the flowers.) Stitch the appliqués onto the brim of the hat, beginning with the bottommost piece of faux rickrack.

Put the flower appliqués on the hat to determine placement, and then stitch each piece onto the hat. Begin with the leaves, then the stems, and finish with the flowers themselves. When adding the flowers, begin stitching in the center, go to the end of the petal, and then backstitch into the center. As a final touch, add a sequin in the center of each flower.

Hat with Wrapped Brim

Although this hat had a great shape and wonderful color, it begged for ornamentation. This novelty yarn—with sparkle and texture—is just the thing. Begin with one ball of novelty yarn, a needle, and clear nylon thread. Wind the yarn around the brim. After three or four revolutions, tack down the yarn at the sides with the clear thread. Continue until the brim is covered as desired, tacking down the yarn every so often. Cut the yarn and bury the loose strand into the yarn. The mohair in this yarn holds the strands together and helps secure the end.

Enhanced Cashmere Scarf

A luxurious scarf becomes even more special with the addition of interesting knit trim. It will no doubt become your favorite winter accessory.

Embellished by Megan Kirby

Materials & Tools

Cashmere scarf

5-inch-wide trim, approximately ⅔ yard

Thread to match the trim

Scissors

Tape measure

Dressmaker's pins

Sewing machine

Instructions

1 If necessary, cut the fringe from the ends of the scarf.

2 Measure the width of the scarf. Cut two pieces of the lace trim to this measurement plus 1 inch.

3 Center the trim on the scarf, right sides together, and pin. You should have an extra ½ inch of trim on either side of the scarf. Stitch the trim to the scarf using a narrow seam allowance.

4 Finish the raw edges of the trim with a narrow hem.

✳ Variation

To create a flirty flounce with lace trim, cut a piece of trim that is roughly twice the width of the scarf, and gather. Pin in place, and stitch as described above. You can add additional ruffled layers as you wish.

Shell with Ribbon Streamers

A group of flowing hand-dyed silk ribbons adds elegance to a silk shell with an attached scarf.

Embellished by Valerie Shrader

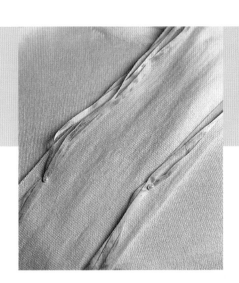

Materials & Tools

Silk knit shell

4mm variegated hand-dyed silk embroidery ribbon in three colors, approximately 3 yards each

Clear nylon thread

10 seed pearls

Tape measure

Scissors

Needles (one sewing needle and one beading needle)

Instructions

1 Determine the length of your streamers and cut two of each color. Make two groups of three ribbons (one of each color) and use the sewing needle to tack them onto the right side of the scarf at a couple of places along its length *but not along the neckline*, because you must be able to pull the shell over your head. (The shell will stretch, but the ribbons will not!) To keep the ribbons in place at the neckline, tack them in one spot only at the side of the neck, using the clear nylon thread.

2 Stitch on the seed pearls with a beading needle, hiding each group of tacking stitches.

3 Repeat steps 1 and 2 to place the second group of ribbons on the scarf.

Gloves with Colorful Trim

Playful trim adds a sense of whimsy to a practical pair of winter gloves.

Embellished by Megan Kirby

Materials & Tools

Knit gloves

Elastic trim, approximately ½ yard

Thread to match the trim

Tape measure

Scissors

Dressmaker's pins

Sewing machine

Instructions

1 Measure the cuff of the gloves and cut two pieces of trim to this measurement plus ¼ inch for overlap.

2 Pin the trim to the gloves, overlapping the edges of the trim. Sew in place using a zigzag stitch. (You can easily stitch by hand as well.)

✳ Variation

A purchased appliqué lends personality to a pair of leather gloves. Simply tack an appliqué to each glove and add a button to hide the stitches.

Fringe-Trimmed Miniskirt

Bold trim and a pair of equally vivacious buttons can completely change the character of a nice (but plain) skirt.

Embellished by Marthe Le Van

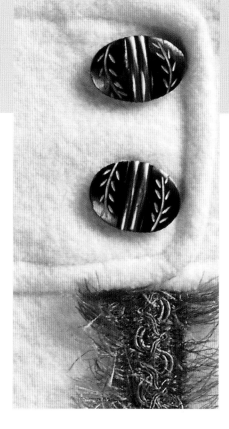

Materials & Tools

Wool skirt

2-inch-wide decorative trim, approximately 2 yards

Thread to match the trim

2 large decorative buttons, each approximately 1¼ inches wide

Dressmaker's pins

Scissors

Needle

Tape measure

Instructions

1 Starting at one side seam of the skirt, pin the trim around the hem. Cut away the excess trim, leaving ½ inch on each end for finishing.

2 Beginning on one edge of the trim, hand stitch it to the skirt, using a needle and matching thread. Stitch the opposite edge in place and remove the pins.

3 Turn under the ends of the trim where they meet at the side seam and hand stitch across both ends from edge to edge.

4 Measure the length of the skirt from the waistband to the hem. Cut a length of trim to this measurement plus 1 inch for finishing. Pin and sew the trim down the front of the skirt, turning under the top edge and tacking in place. Turn under the bottom edge of the trim and tack it to the wrong side of the skirt.

5 Place the decorative buttons on the front of the skirt as you wish and sew in place.

Appliquéd Linen Dress

This comfortable linen dress was a bit too long for summer wear.
A knee-length hem and some ethnic accents made it just right for the season.

Embellished by Brooke Dickson

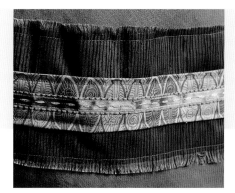

Materials & Tools

Linen dress

2 pieces of complementary fabric, approximately ¼ yard each

1 roll of ½-inch-wide decorative ribbon

Thread in contrasting color to the fabrics

Tape measure

Dressmaker's pencil

Scissors

Sewing machine

Iron

Dressmaker's pins

Instructions

1 If your dress is too long for your taste, determine the desired length of the dress. Mark the new length and cut. Hem the edge.

2 Measure the width of the front of the dress and cut one of the pieces of fabric to this measurement by 5 inches wide. To produce a raveled edge, pull loose threads horizontally across the fabric. Cut the ribbon to the same length as this fabric.

3 Cut the second fabric a few inches shorter than the piece you cut in step 2, and only about 3 inches wide. Turn under the raw edges along the length of this piece and press; do not finish the edges along the width.

4 Use the contrasting thread for steps 4 and 5. Pin the wider piece of fabric onto the dress and stitch in place along each edge. Center the narrower fabric on top and stitch.

5 Center the ribbon on the printed fabric and sew it in place, turning under the raw edges.

Lacy Camisole

Bring a decidedly feminine touch to this camisole by attaching lace and weaving in a delicate ribbon.

Embellished by Carey Baker

Materials & Tools

Rayon/polyester camisole with V-neck

3-inch-wide lace, approximately 1 yard

¼-inch-wide ribbon, approximately 1⅔ yards

Thread to match the shirt and the lace

Tape measure

Scissors

Dressmaker's pins

Sewing machine

Tapestry needle

Instructions

1 Measure the front neckline of the camisole and cut a piece of lace to this measurement. Measure the front of the camisole at the hem and cut a piece of lace to this measurement, adding an extra inch to turn under the raw edges.

2 Pin the smaller piece of lace inside the neckline and sew it in place using thread that matches the camisole. Trim the excess lace on the inside of the shirt.

3 Turn under the raw edges of the remaining piece of lace and stitch, using the thread that matches the lace. Pin the lace along the hem and stitch it in place, using the thread that matches the top.

4 Beginning in the center of the camisole at the waistline, use the tapestry needle to weave the ribbon in and out in a running stitch. Tie small knots at the ends of the ribbon and trim the excess.

Embroidered White Dress

A little color is all that is needed to add visual interest to this smart dress with princess seams. Choose some complementary colors of floss for a quick and easy makeover.

Embellished by Valerie Shrader

Materials & Tools

Wool/rayon knit dress

Embroidery floss in three
complementary colors,
1 skein each

Embroidery needle

Instructions

1 See Embroidery Techniques on page 124 for embroidery
stitch directions; begin by adding woven wheels around
the neckline of the dress, alternating the colors. Add a
French knot in the center of each wheel, using a contrasting
color.

2 Using the armhole hemline as a guide, make a row of
running stitches along each arm opening. Place a row of
French knots above the first row of running stitches,
using a second color of floss. Finish with another row of running stitches that parallels the first row, using the remaining
color of floss. Add embroidery at the hem, if desired.

✳ Note

Embroidery can be a valuable skill in embellishing
clothing, and even the simplest stitch can add charm and
sophistication.

Decorated Skirt

Compliments will abound when you wear this classic A-line skirt
adorned with ribbons and trim, accented with decorative stitching.

Embellished by Kelledy Francis

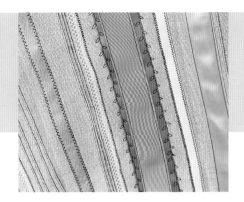

Materials & Tools

Linen skirt

Assortment of trim (including ribbon and hem tape), approximately 2 yards each

Machine embroidery thread in a contrasting color to the skirt

Tape measure

Scissors

Dressmaker's pins

Sewing machine

Machine embroidery needle

Embroidery presser foot (if required)

Pintucking presser foot

Machine double needle

Instructions

1 Measure the length of your skirt and cut each piece of trim to that length, adding an extra 1 inch to turn under the raw edges.

2 Pin the trim to the front of the skirt, folding the raw edges under at the waistband. At the hem, fold under the raw edges and tack to the wrong side of the skirt. Create some custom trim by layering one ribbon atop another as desired.

3 Use various decorative and zigzag stitches to attach all the trim.

4 Add pintucks to fill in the areas between the trim.

✳ Note

If you don't have a pintucking foot for your sewing machine, you can mimic this look by simply making parallel rows of straight stitches. Likewise, if your machine doesn't offer many embroidery stitches, use a variety of zigzag and straight stitches at varying widths and lengths.

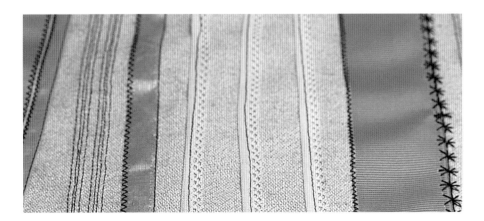

Sweater with Woven Accents

If an indispensable sweater in your closet could use some extra attention, accentuate the hem and cuffs with a bit of wool yarn and bright ribbon.

Embellished by Brooke Dickson

Materials & Tools

Cotton sweater

1 ball of yarn in a complementary color to the sweater

1 roll of ⅜-inch-wide ribbon in a complementary color to the yarn

2 rolls of ⅛-inch-wide ribbon in a complementary color to the yarn

Tape measure

Scissors

Tapestry needle

Instructions

1 Measure the hem's circumference and cut a piece of yarn slightly longer than this measurement. Using the tapestry needle, weave over one row of knitting, then under the next row, all around the hem. Make a second revolution just above the first row, alternating the placement of the stitches. Tie the ends of the yarn together on the wrong side of the sweater.

2 Thread the tapestry needle with the wide ribbon and weave over three rows of knitting, then under one row, just above the yarn you added in step 1. Tie the ribbon ends together as in step 1.

3 Thread the narrow ribbon through the tapestry needle and weave vertically at random heights. Continue around the sweater and tie the ribbon ends together as in step 1.

4 Repeat the pattern from steps 1 through 3 at each cuff.

Sequined Scarf

This scarf is decorated to eliminate a "wrong" side where the stitching would show. Each end of the scarf showcases a variation of this technique.

Embellished by Valerie Shrader

Materials & Tools

Wool challis scarf

Vintage sequins in three colors, one color larger than the other two

Embroidery floss to match the colors of the sequins, 1 skein each

Embroidery needle (sized to fit through the eyes of the sequins)

Scissors

Instructions

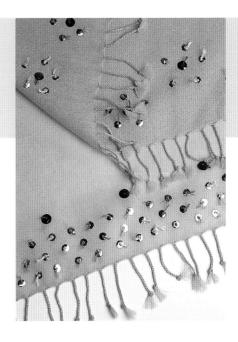

1 This simple technique consists of knotting the floss and inserting the needle down through the front of the sequin to the other side of the scarf. Insert the needle through the back of a sequin on the other side, knot the floss, and cut the end. The sequins look exactly the same on either side of the scarf (see photo at the right).

2 One end of the scarf features alternating triangles of sequins made from the two colors of smaller sequins. To re-create this effect, stitch on the sequins as described in step 1 and follow this pattern seen in the photo at the right.

1st row: 3 sequins in one color, 1 sequin in the second color, repeat to the end of the row.

2nd row (beginning above the space between the first two sequins in the 1st row): 2 sequins of the first color, 2 sequins of the second color, repeat to the end of the row.

3rd row (beginning above the space between the first two sequins of the 2nd row): 1 sequin of the first color, 3 sequins of the second color, repeat to the end of the row. Add a final row of the large sequins, placing them above the single sequin of the first color in the top row.

3 The opposite end of the scarf features a scattering of sequins in a circular pattern. Using the method described in step 1, first stitch on 6 large sequins. Then surround each large sequin with a group of 5 smaller sequins.

✳ Note

The matte silver sequins in this project were enhanced by silk embroidery floss.

✳ Variation

For alternative ways to attach sequins, see Sequin Techniques on page 121.

Linen Blouse with Pintucking

Colorful decorative stitching and pintucking add character and charm to any blouse. New buttons in a complementary color complete the transformation.

Embellished by Kelledy Francis

Materials & Tools

Linen blouse

Rayon machine embroidery thread

6 buttons in a complementary color, each approximately ⅜ inch wide

Dressmaker's pins

Tear-away stabilizer

Sewing machine

Machine double needle

Pintucking presser foot

Machine embroidery needle

Embroidery presser foot (if required)

Instructions

1 Pin the tear-away stabilizer to the wrong side of the blouse where the embroidery will be.

2 Begin with the front of the blouse and determine where you want the pintucking to begin. Stitch the first row. Use this row as a guide as you add the next rows of decorative stitches. Repeat the pattern of stitches on the other side of the blouse.

3 For added effect, use a combination of pintucking and stitches on the cuffs. Add a decorative row of pintucks around the collar.

4 Replace the original buttons with those in a complementary hue to the embellishment. Remove the stabilizer, following the manufacturer's instructions.

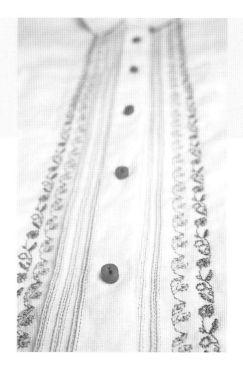

Dress with Flowing Scarf

This classic sheath radiates style and whimsy with an organdy scarf that is decorated with plush polka dots. The scarf drapes to the back of the dress, providing drama from every angle.

Embellished by Valerie Shrader

Materials & Tools

Cotton dress

Embellished organdy, approximately ¾ yard

Thread to match the organdy

Thread to match the ribbon

⅜-inch-wide velvet ribbon, approximately 1¼ yards

Scissors

Tape measure

Dressmaker's pins

Sewing machine

Needle

Instructions

1 Construct this scarf from two pieces of fabric. Decide on the total length of your scarf, divide that measurement in half, and cut out two pieces of organdy that are each this length by approximately 10 inches wide. (For example, this scarf measures about 88 inches, so it was cut as two 44- x 10-inch sections.)

2 Pin each individual section into a tube, right sides together. Stitch using a narrow seam allowance. Turn each section right side out.

When replicating this project, look for a simple dress with a neckline that offers some excitement, such as this deep V-neck design. Make sure that the fabric you choose for the scarf has enough body to enhance the neckline.

3 Place the two sections together, right sides facing, and stitch together using a narrow seam allowance. (This seam will fall in the center front of the dress and be hidden by a velvet carrier.)

4 Since this fabric was 44 inches wide, the scarf was cut so the selvages were placed at the ends. If you have raw edges exposed, finish them as desired and then cut two pieces of velvet ribbon to the circumference of the tube. With the needle and matching thread, backstitch the ribbon to the ends of the scarf, covering the hem (or the selvage) as appropriate.

5 Make loops of velvet ribbon to hold the scarf in place. Cut three loops that are each about 3 inches in length. (These measurements could vary depending on your garment.) To make the loop in the center of the neckline, turn under the raw edges and tack into place. To make the loops at the shoulder seams, wrap the pieces of ribbon around the shoulder, turn under the raw edges, and whipstitch the ends together on the wrong side of the garment. To hold the loops in place, be sure to catch a few threads of the dress as you whipstitch.

6 Measure the waist of the dress and cut a length of ribbon to this measurement, adding ½ inch to turn under the raw edges. Turn under these raw edges as you stitch the ribbon in place at each side of the zipper in the back of the dress.

7 Using the thread that matches the color of the ribbon, make belt carriers for the ribbon ties at the side seams. (In couture sewing, you may see a belt carrier referred to as a *thread bar*.) Use your favorite method to make a belt carrier, or create one like so: Use the ribbon as a guide while you stitch through the dress from the wrong side and loop the thread loosely around the ribbon by stitching down through the dress on the other side of the ribbon. Make another loop or two around the ribbon. Bring the needle back to the right side of the fabric, hold the loops together, and cover them with a series of blanket stitches, working the entire length of the loops from one side to the other (figure 1). To finish, insert the needle back through the dress and knot on the wrong side. The carriers will keep the ribbon belt in place. (For more information on belt carriers, see Sewing Techniques on page 120.)

Figure 1

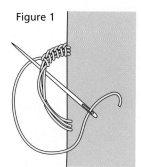

Wispy Macramé Cuffs

Strands of silk ribbon whisper around your wrists, dressing up this simple T-shirt.
Add pony beads for further decoration.

Embellished by Terry Taylor

Materials & Tools

Cotton knit T-shirt with three-quarter length sleeves

Foam core board, 6 x 6 inches

4mm silk embroidery ribbon in three colors, approximately 3 yards of each per sleeve

4mm pony beads, approximately 3 dozen

Craft knife

Ruler or tape measure

Dressmaker's pencil

Scissors

Embroidery needle

T-pins

Instructions

1   Using a craft knife, cut the foam core board to the width of the sleeve cuff. Mark four or five horizontal lines on the board at approximately 1-inch intervals.

2   Cut the silk ribbon into approximately 18-inch lengths.

3   Slip the foam core board into one sleeve cuff. Make marks at ½-inch intervals around the circumference of the cuff.

4   Thread the needle with one end of the silk ribbon and insert it into the cuff. Pull the ribbon through the cuff, and then slip it off the needle. Gently tug on the ribbon to make the ends even. Repeat the process around the cuff at each marked spot.

5   Join the adjacent ribbons with square knots (figure 1). To keep the knots even, make an overhand knot, place a T-pin on the first line of the foam core board, and then finish the knot by tightening it against the pin. Repeat across the cuff. Turn the cuff over and work around the back.

6   Join the adjacent ribbons with knots at the second line of the board. Leave the first row of pins in as you work, inserting a row of pins as you work the second row. After working the second row, remove the first row of pins.

7   Knot three or four rows around the cuff, as desired.

8   Thread one pony bead onto the two ribbons used to make the last row of knots. Secure the bead with another square knot. Repeat around the cuff.

9   Repeat steps 3 through 8 for the second cuff.

✳ Note

This designer used three different colors of silk ribbon for a variegated effect. If you prefer, you can purchase variegated silk ribbon.

Figure 1

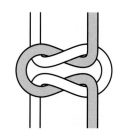

Variations on a Theme: Cashmere Sweater

A fabulous sale find, this exquisite sweater has a bateau neckline that lends itself beautifully to a variety of decorative techniques. Each is easily created, and the embellishment can be changed at your whim.

Appliqués

These appliqués from a specialty trim shop feature couched beads, iridescent paillettes, and seed pearls. Simply tack them in place as desired, using clear nylon thread.

Beaded Trim

A length of spectacular beaded trim makes the ultimate embellishment. To create this look, find a trim that closely matches the width of the neckline; you'll also need a pair of scissors, a needle, and clear nylon thread. Measure the neckline and cut the trim accordingly, allowing an extra 1 inch or so for the overlap.

Since you are stitching an item with no elasticity (the trim) to the knit sweater, stitch the trim on as follows to compensate for its lack of stretch: Sew on the trim with a whipstitch just a few inches at a time, sewing on the bottom edge of the trim at the bodice first, then easing the sweater onto the top edge of the trim as you stitch along the neckline. (A bit of stretch in the neckline will inevitably be lost.)

Narrowly turn under the raw edges of trim and whipstitch them together when you finish, cutting the length of beaded trim as necessary.

Collage

Make a collage of the following materials: silk and organza ribbons, vintage mother-of-pearl buttons, sequins, and purchased silk flowers. You'll also need thread, a needle, and maybe some silk pins. Begin with three strands of ribbon in unequal lengths. Use colorful thread to secure them under a button near the shoulder, and then let them meander from button to button across the neckline, tacking down the ribbon as you sew on each button. Pin the ribbons in place, if necessary, using silk pins. Scatter the other embellishments as desired.

Pompoms

For the sheer joy of it, enliven the neckline with yarn pompoms. You'll need the following tools and supplies: three or four yarns of varying texture and color; a pair of scissors; a yarn needle; and a piece of sturdy

cardboard or card stock. Cut a square of cardboard that is half the width of your finished pompom and notch two opposing sides. Gather the yarns together and wrap them tightly around the notch as shown; the more you wrap, the more dense your pompom.

Cut a length of yarn about 6 inches long and thread it into the yarn needle. Insert the needle under the bundle of yarn on one side of the cardboard; pull the strand under so you have equal lengths on either side of the bundle. Tie the 6-inch length of yarn together very tightly and cut through the bundle on the opposite side of the cardboard. Trim the ends as desired; in these pompoms the ends of the yarn bundle were kept deliberately long, as was the yarn tie.

Velvet-Trimmed Knit Tank

A little velvet ribbon and some complementary buttons are all
that's needed to add a little personality to this ribbed tank.

Embellished by Carey Baker

Materials & Tools

Cotton knit tank

⅜-inch-wide elastic velvet trim, approximately 2 yards

Thread to match the trim

1 button, approximately ¾ inch wide

4 buttons, approximately ¼ inch wide

Tape measure

Scissors

Sewing machine

Seam ripper

Needle

Instructions

1 Measure the neck and armholes of the tank top and cut three pieces of the velvet trim to these measurements; add a scant ⅛ inch for overlap.

2 Beginning at one shoulder seam, baste the longer piece of trim along the neckline.

3 Adjust the stitch length and stitch as close as possible to the edges of the trim and across the overlapping end.

4 Repeat this process with the armholes, beginning at the side seam.

5 Use a seam ripper to remove the basting stitches.

6 Sew the large button onto the trim at the center of the neckline. Sew two of the smaller buttons on each side of the large button.

Ruffled Skirt

Feminine, flirty ruffles offer the perfect antidote to the plain skirt.
Use a combination of fabrics and contrasting thread to add color and texture.

Embellished by Valerie Shrader

Materials & Tools

Cotton skirt

4 complementary fabrics, approximately ¼ yard each

Roll of fusible bonding web (optional)

Cutting mat

Rotary cutter

Quilter's see-through ruler

Sewing machine

Iron (optional)

Dressmaker's pins

Seam ripper

Scissors

Instructions

1 Assemble each ruffle for the skirt from strips of the different fabrics. The total length of the ruffles before gathering should be approximately twice the length of the skirt. For instance, the ruffles on this skirt were 40 inches long, and thus each ruffle consisted of four 10-inch pieces of fabric, each 2 inches wide. To make the cutting fast and easy, use a cutting mat, rotary cutter, and quilter's ruler.

2 After you decide on the fabric arrangement for each ruffle, stitch them together as you

add the line of basting stitches down the center of the ruffle. Overlap each piece about ½ inch as you baste (see the example below). Because this embellishment is designed to appear slightly decon- structed, you don't need to finish the raw edges before you overlap.

3 Roughly finish the edges of the ruffles with satin stitching. (Make a satin stitch by setting your sewing machine to a zigzag setting and a very short length, so the stitches are very close together.) Let the right side of the zigzag stitch fall off the edge of the fabric, and the edge will roll to be some- what encased by the stitch. If you have a serger, it can also be used to finish the edges.

4 Turn under the raw edges at either end of the ruffle and secure with bonding web, if desired, removing a few of the basting stitches to allow the ends to be folded. Gather each ruffle by pulling the basting thread. Pin in place along the front of the skirt; this skirt had panels, so the ruffles were placed along the seamlines.

Adjust the gathers for balance. Fold the bottom of the ruffle to the wrong side of the skirt. Baste to the skirt, and then stitch in place.

5 Remove the basting stitches. For visual emphasis, stitch again over the existing seamline.

6 Make a fabric corsage for the waistline. Use your favorite method, or construct it in lay- ers as follows: Cut the largest bot- tom layer in a circle and clip to the center. Cut out a small circle in the center. Finish the edges with satin stitch as described in step 3. Make a row of basting stitches around the center opening, and pull to gather. Pin to the skirt, adjusting the gathers as necessary. Baste in place around the center.

7 Cut two smaller circles. If desired, finish the edges as described in step 3. Layer them, and fold in quarters (in half, then in half again at the center). Hand stitch through all the layers at the center point. Pin in place in the center of the fabric circle applied in step 6.

✳ Note

Resist the temptation to face these ruffles—the added layer of fabric will not gather readily.

When shopping for complementary fabrics for a project such as this one, consider a shop that specializes in quilting fabrics. Quite often, their fabrics are arranged according to colorway (and not fiber content), so you can quickly and easily find what you want.

Ribbon-Wrapped Shrug

If a favorite sweater is no longer au courant, transform it into something chic. This sweater has been reconstructed and adorned with a combination of ribbon and decorative stitching.

Embellished by Valerie Shrader

Materials & Tools

Merino wool wrap sweater

2⅛-inch-wide organza ribbon, approximately 1 yard

Thread in a contrasting color to the ribbon

⅜-inch-wide grosgrain ribbon in a complementary color to the organza ribbon, approximately 1½ yards

Hook-and-loop tape (optional)

Tape measure

Silk pins

Scissors

Sewing machine

Instructions

1 Turn this sweater into a shrug by first measuring and marking with pins where the sweater should be shortened. Carefully trim away the bottom of the sweater.

2 Measure and cut the organza ribbon to the width of the sweater, including the overlap. Pin the wide organza along the bottom of the sweater, leaving about ½ inch to be turned under to enclose the cut edge. Ease the sweater to fit. Stitch along the upper edge of the ribbon with contrasting thread. Fold the bottom edge to the inside and stitch. Fold under the raw edges of the ribbon and whipstitch to the wrong side of the shrug.

3 Try on the sweater. Use a pin to mark the spot on the left side of the sweater that's 1 inch or so away from the overlap. (This sweater overlaps right to left.) You will end the stitching at this spot when you stitch on the grosgrain ribbon tie in the next step.

4 Cut the grosgrain ribbon to the desired length; remember that this ribbon will be the tie closure, so include sufficient length for this purpose. Place the grosgrain on top of the organza, extending equal amounts on each side for the ties (at least 12 inches). On the right side of the sweater (that wraps to the outside), begin stitching the grosgrain to the organza, placing it in the center of the larger ribbon. Use a decorative stitch and the contrasting thread. On the left side of the sweater, stitch to the point that you marked in step 3 (see the photo above).

5 Measure the circumference of the cuffs and add several inches. Cut two pieces of organza ribbon to this size and stitch one to each cuff with a narrow zigzag stitch, overlapping the excess ribbon.

6 If desired, stitch hook-and-loop tape on the inside of the sweater where the two sides overlap.

Free-Motion Shirt

Fully express your sense of creativity by embellishing a shirt with free-motion machine embroidery. This technique allows you to draw with the sewing machine.

Embellished by Kelledy Francis

Materials & Tools

Cotton/spandex shirt

Rayon machine embroidery thread

Metallic machine embroidery thread

Dressmaker's pencil or iron-on transfer design

Embroidery hoop

Tear-away stabilizer

Dressmaker's pins

Sewing machine

Machine embroidery needle

Free-motion embroidery (darning) presser foot

Instructions

1 Use a dressmaker's pencil to sketch a design on the front of the shirt. Alternatively, use an iron-on transfer design, following the manufacturer's instructions.

2 Place the shirt in the embroidery hoop, with tear-away stabilizer pinned on the wrong side of the fabric under the design. The fabric should be positioned in the hoop so it lies flat against the sewing machine bed; do this by placing the right side of the fabric over the hoop's outer ring and then position the inner ring.

3 Using the proper accessories for your sewing machine and a machine embroidery needle, lower the feed dogs and set the stitch width to zero. Stitch over the design you applied in step 1, changing thread as desired.

4 If desired, add free-motion embroidery to the cuffs and topstitch along the placket, collar, and cuffs.

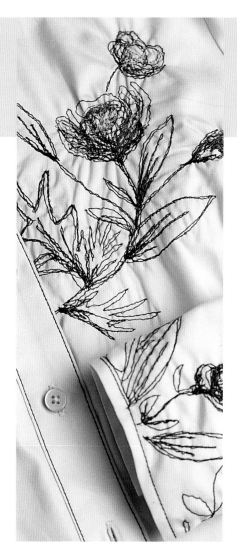

✳ Note

Most sewing machines can be used for free-motion embroidery if they are equipped with the proper accessories. Check the manual from your machine for more information.

Tulle-Trimmed Tank Top

Tulle is a graceful complement to the variety of trims used on this tank top.

Embellished by Nathalie Mornu

Materials & Tools

Cotton knit tank top

Tulle in a complementary color to the top, approximately 2 yards

5-inch-wide trim, approximately 1 yard

1¾-inch-wide gathered trim, approximately 1½ yards

⅜-inch-wide decorative elastic trim, approximately 3 yards

Tape measure

Dressmaker's pencil or water-soluble marking pen

Sewing machine

Scissors

Dressmaker's pins

Iron

Instructions

1 If the tank top hangs low on the hips, crop it just below the waist by first measuring and marking the length. Run a line of zigzag stitching along the marked line to prevent fraying and cut off the excess fabric.

2 Measure the front of the top at the hem and cut four pieces of tulle to this measurement by 6 inches wide.

3 Extend the 5-inch-wide trim ½ inch beyond one side seam (to turn under the raw edges later) and pin it to the bottom of the tank top, right sides together. Once you've pinned it all the way around, cut off any excess trim, leaving a ½ inch on the opposite end. Baste. Layer two pieces of tulle and pin them on top of the trim on the front of the tank top, layering one strip exactly on top of the other. Match the side edges of the tulle to the side seams of the top. Repeat on the back, and then stitch in place. Turn and press carefully. Finish the raw edges of the trim with a narrow hem; leave the tulle as is.

4 Measure and mark the placement of the gathered trim. In this project, one strip was placed high on the chest and the other 3 inches above the hem. Starting at one side seam, pin the gathered trim in place on the right side of the shirt. Once it's pinned all the way around, leave ½ inch for overlap and cut off the excess. Turn the raw edge under and overlap the other end of the trim.

5 Pin the elastic trim so its decorative edges face away from the gathered trim, covering the edges of the gathered trim. (Be careful not to stretch the elastic.) Turn under the raw edges and pin. Use a zigzag stitch to sew the elastic and the trim at the same time.

Velvet-Wrapped Dress

Accentuate the flattering lines of this knit dress by adding a body-hugging tie of stretch velvet. Beads and sequins add an extra bit of flair.

Embellished by Valerie Shrader

Materials & Tools

Silk/rayon knit dress

⅜-inch-wide vintage stretch velvet ribbon, approximately 2⅔ yards

Clear nylon thread

Thread to match the ribbon

Seed beads in three complementary colors, 1 tube each (optional)

Sequins (optional)

Beading thread (optional)

Silk pins

Scissors

Needle

Beading needle (optional)

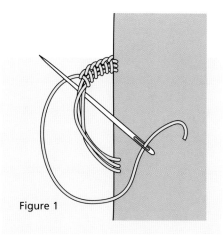

Figure 1

Instructions

1 Determine the length of your ties by trying on the dress. Carefully pin the ribbon in place, and then cut the ties to the desired length.

2 Hand stitch the ribbon to the dress as necessary, using the clear nylon thread. In this project, the ribbon was stitched down along the neckline only.

3 Using the thread that matches the ribbon, make belt carriers at the side seams. Use your favorite method to make a belt carrier or create one like so (figure 1): Use the ribbon as a guide while you stitch through the dress and loop the thread loosely around the ribbon a few times. Bring the needle back to the right side of the fabric, hold the loops together, and cover them with a series of blanket stitches, working from one side to the other. To finish, insert the needle back through the dress and knot on the wrong side. The carriers will keep the ribbon ties in place. (For more information on belt carriers, see Sewing Techniques on page 120.)

4 If desired, add bead and sequin embellishments, using the fabric's print as a guide. This project features several groups of beaded embellishments made from single-needle couching and lazy stitch, as well as sequins with bead centers. (See Beading Techniques on page 122 for more information.)

White Blouse with Black Ribbon Trim

Accent a plain blouse with simple ribbon and button embellishments. A blouse with details such as tucking offers easy lines to follow.

Embellished by Joan K. Morris

Materials & Tools

Linen wrap blouse

⅛-inch-wide ribbon, approximately 7 yards

Fabric glue

Thread to match the ribbon

17 buttons with shanks, each approximately ¾ inch wide

Tape measure

Scissors

Sewing machine

Water-soluble marking pen

Needle

Instructions

1 Decide where you want to place the ribbon. This wrap blouse offered easy access to all areas, so the neckline, hem, and sleeves were embellished, and ribbon was added between the tucks at the waistline.

2 To begin, measure around the neckline and cut a piece of ribbon to that measurement plus an extra inch. To keep this thin ribbon from unraveling, fold under the ends and apply the fabric glue to bond in place. Let dry.

3 To apply the ribbon an equal distance from the edges of the blouse, use the measurement marks on your sewing machine's needle plate. (For example, this ribbon was sewn on following the ¾-inch mark.) Stitch the ribbon in place with matching thread.

4 Add the horizontal lines of ribbon between the existing tucks in the blouse. If you don't have an existing design to follow, draw lines with a marking pen. Prepare these pieces of ribbon as instructed in step 2.

5 Sew on the accent buttons as desired. To hide the knots, place them on the right side of the blouse, where the buttons will cover them.

Linen Skirt with Lace Insets

The diagonal panels on this skirt lend themselves beautifully to the addition of lace, set into the slashed seams. Use a variety of ribbon accents for the finishing touches.

Embellished by Valerie Shrader

Materials & Tools

Handkerchief linen skirt

3-inch-wide lace, approximately 1 yard

Thread to match the skirt

⅜-inch-wide ribbon, in at least two complementary colors, approximately 2 yards of each color

Seam ripper

Tape measure

Scissors

Iron

Silk pins

Needle

Sewing machine

Instructions

1 Use the seam ripper to remove a few inches of the skirt's hem surrounding the diagonal seams, and then remove the seams to the desired point. Measure to this point and cut the lace to this length plus 1 extra inch. Press under each seam allowance on the skirt and place the lace under the opened seams; pull apart the seams to the width desired as you pin the lace in place. Hand baste the lace to the skirt.

2 Measure the length of your slashed seams and cut ribbon for each side of the slash to this measurement; in this project, one color of ribbon extends from the hem to the waistband on the left side of the slash, following the seamline. The remaining color highlights the right side of the slash and the waistband. Allow ½ inch extra to turn under the ends at the hem.

3 Pin the ribbon in place along the slashed seam, covering the basting stitches, and let the ribbon from the left side of the slash overlap the ribbon on the right side as shown. Sew in place, using a zigzag or decorative stitch as desired. Use contrasting thread if you wish.

4 Turn under the raw edges of the lace and ribbon as you re-stitch the narrow hem. Measure and cut a length of ribbon for the waistband; pin and stitch in place, being sure to cover the raw edges of the ribbon that extend along the diagonal seamline.

Skirt with Woven Ribbons

This simple technique can be used on practically any garment to allow the weaving of ribbon or trim. Complement your garment with ribbons of several colors.

Embellished by Valerie Shrader

Materials & Tools

Polyester knit skirt

Ribbon in varying colors
and widths, approximately
1 yard each

Thread to match the skirt

Lightweight tear-away stabilizer
(optional)

Tape measure

Scissors

Water-soluble fabric marker

Sewing machine

Cutting mat

Craft knife or seam ripper

Needle

Instructions

1 Measure the front of the skirt and cut lengths of each ribbon to this measurement plus an extra 9 or 10 inches to tie the bow.

2 Using the width of each ribbon as a guide, mark spots for the buttonholes along the skirt. Begin with a single buttonhole at the side seam, from which the ribbon will emerge to the right side of the skirt, and then mark pairs of buttonholes across to the other side seam.

3 Make the buttonholes by machine or by hand, placing squares of stabilizer under each buttonhole, if necessary. Place the skirt on the cutting mat and slash the center of each buttonhole with the craft knife or seam ripper.

4 On the wrong side of the skirt, stitch one end of each ribbon to the seam nearest the single buttonhole. Bring the ribbon out to the right side of the skirt through the single buttonhole and pass it through each pair of buttonholes. Bring each ribbon to a common point at the far seam and tack in place.

5 Cut additional lengths of ribbon that are approximately 20 inches long. Make a bow from these lengths of ribbon and tie in place on the skirt, using the lengths of ribbon attached to the skirt.

Capelet with Crocheted Edging

This freeform edging, using the most rudimentary crochet stitch, is quite easy, and the eyelash yarn disguises uneven stitches while being both fuzzy *and* frilly.

Embellished by Terry Taylor

Materials & Tools

Wool/acrylic capelet

Thread to match the capelet

1 skein of bulky eyelash yarn

Needles (one sewing needle
and one tapestry needle)

Crochet hook, 5 to 6mm
(size H to J U.S.)

Figure 1

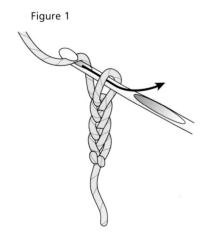

Instructions

1 Whipstitch around the edge of
the neckline with a doubled
length of sewing thread. Make
your stitches approximately ⅜ inch
long. Don't pull them too tightly if
you are working on knit material.

2 Find the end of your yarn. Use
the crochet hook to pull up a
short loop through one of your
whipstitches, leaving several inches
of yarn free. Insert your hook down
into the next whipstitch. Catch the
yarn from the skein with the hook.
Use the hook to pull up the yarn
through the whipstitch and the first
loop. You've completed one chain
stitch. (See figure 1; for more information, see Crochet Techniques on
page 121).

3 Work your way around the
neckline, inserting your hook
into a whipstitch and pulling
up the yarn to make a chain stitch.
When you return to the beginning,
work a chain stitch into the very
first stitch to join the chain. This is
your foundation chain.

4 Make a length of 10 to 15
chain stitches. With the last
chain on your hook, insert the
hook back into the foundation chain
close to where you began, catch the
yarn with your hook and pull it
through the loop on your hook.
You've made one edging loop.

5 Repeat step 4 all around the
garment. Vary the length of
your chains—some shorter and
some longer.

6 When you have worked your
way around the garment once,
keep crocheting as you wish.
You may work more edging loops
into the foundation chain or make
chains and join them to the first
round of edging loops. Weave in
the yarn ends when you are satis-
fied with the edging.

Sequined Skirt

Vintage sequins provide the perfect flair for this already stunning skirt.
Layers of netting, attached to the crinoline underskirt, add drama and movement.

Embellished by Nathalie Mornu

Materials & Tools

Silk skirt

Decorative netting, approximately ½ yard

Thread to match the skirt

⅜-inch-wide vintage sequins, approximately 75

Tape measure

Scissors

Dressmaker's pins

Sewing machine

Needle

Instructions

1 When this skirt was purchased, it had an attached crinoline underskirt. The flounce added in this project was sewn to the underskirt instead of the hem of the skirt. To begin, decide on the length of your flounce and adjust for any additional length between the underskirt and the hemline. The netting in this project hangs about 2 inches below the hem.

2 Measure the circumference of the hemline and cut strips of netting to equal twice this measurement by the length you chose in step 1. (For example, strips were sewn together in this project to equal 4 inches long by 120 inches wide.)

3 Gather the strip of netting and pin it to the wrong side of the underskirt. Stitch.

4 Randomly sew the vintage sequins to the skirt, placing more sequins near the hem. Use a doubled strand of thread and stitch through the sequin twice for security.

* Note

If you have a similar skirt, but it does not have an underskirt, simply stitch the flounce to the wrong side of the skirt's hem.

Shirt with Beaded Tucks

Transform a somewhat shapeless shirt into an elegant blouse shimmering
with beadwork. Create visual interest with a series of tucks and a scalloped hem.

Embellished by Joan K. Morris

Materials & Tools

Silk shirt

Roll of fusible bonding web

Thread to match the shirt

Bugle beads, approximately 150

Clear beading thread

Scrap paper for template

6 glass buttons, each
approximately ¼ inch wide

Tape measure

Scissors (one pair fabric and one
pair craft)

Iron and ironing board

Dressmaker's pins

Sewing machine

Needle

Beading needle

Pencil

Instructions

1 Using fabric scissors, cut off the
sleeves of the shirt approximately 1 inch from the sleeve
seam. Save the sleeves to use in
step 9.

4 About every 3 inches, pull the tucks together and whipstitch. This will create six sections on each side of the shirt.

5 To create the diamond motif, open up each section and whipstitch it to the shirt. Press the diamonds open.

6 Backstitch a row of bugle beads in the center of each diamond motif, using the clear thread and the beading needle. (See figure 1; for more information, see Beading Techniques on page 122).

7 Make a template to create the scalloped hem. Begin by measuring around the hem of the shirt and add 4 inches. (This extra length will allow you to move the template around and find the best placement on the shirt.) Using craft scissors, cut a piece of paper that is the length of your measurement by 4 inches wide. Mark a spot every 4 inches along one edge and connect the dots with half circles that are the width of the paper. Cut out the template. (Alternatively, you could use a French curve to mark the scallops.)

8 Place the template on the shirt, scalloped edge along the hem, and position as desired. Cut the excess length of the pattern, leaving an extra inch at each end.

2 Turn the shirt inside out. Fold and press the remaining sleeve to the inside to serve as a facing. Follow the manufacturer's instructions and use the bonding web to adhere the sleeve facing.

3 To create the tucked design, you will make a set of tucks on each side of the shirt. To begin, measure approximately 1½ inches from the center of the shirt and ½ inch down from the shoulder seam. Make a small fold of fabric beginning at this spot and pin it in place all the way down the front. Stitch as close as you can to the edge of the fold. Repeat to create a second fold that is about 1½ inches from the first. Repeat this step to make the tucks on the other side of the shirt.

9 Use the sleeves to create the facing for the hem. Cut the sleeves along the lengthwise seam; stitch the two sleeves together using a ½-inch seam allowance and create a long piece of fabric. Pin the template in place and cut out the fabric. Turn under the straight edge and make a narrow machine hem.

10 If your shirt has a wide hem, let it out and place the scalloped edge of the facing just above the hemline, right sides together. Pin and stitch around the scalloped facing using a ½-inch seam allowance, pivoting at the points.

11 Trim the seam and clip the curves; clip to the point of each scallop. Turn the facing to the inside and press in place. Fold under the center front edges of the facing and the shirt, press, and pin together. Whipstitch the edges closed.

12 Use bonding web to fuse the hem to the shirt. Replace the original buttons with glass buttons.

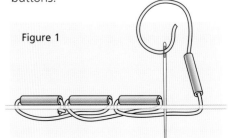

Figure 1

Shirt with Silk Flounces

Transform a lackluster dress shirt by adding silk accents and new buttons—
not to mention a fabulous silk flower.

Embellished by Jen Swearington

Materials & Tools

Cotton/spandex shirt with three-quarter length sleeves

5 buttons to complement the fabric, each approximately ½ inch wide

Thread to match the shirt

Silk fabric for sleeve extensions and cuffs, approximately ½ yard

Bias binding, made from approximately 1 additional yard of silk, *or* ½-inch-wide bias tape, approximately ½ yard

Seam ripper

Needle

Tape measure

Scissors

Pins

Sewing machine

Iron

Small safety pin

Instructions

1 Using a seam ripper, remove the original buttons and replace them with the new buttons.

2 If the existing sleeves have slits, whipstitch them together.

3 You will make a sleeve extension and a flounce in this project. To begin, try on the shirt and measure from the end of the existing sleeve to your wrist. This is the total measurement for the sleeve extension and the flounce.

4 To make the sleeve extension, use the measurement from step 3 and subtract the length of the flounce. Add 1 inch to the length for the seam allowances. (For example, the total length in this project was 8 inches, and the flounce was 2 inches. So the sleeve extension was 6 inches plus 1 inch for the seam allowances to equal 7 inches.)

5 Measure the circumference of the existing cuff and add 1 inch for the side seam allowance. Cut a piece of silk fabric to this measurement by the length you figured in step 4.

6 To make the flounce for the cuff, you will cut a circle of silk fabric, make a slit to the center, and remove a portion of the center so the piece resembles a doughnut (figure 1). The fabric left in the circle should be the length you determined in step 1 plus a ½-inch seam allowance. (For example, in this project, the circle was cut 10 inches in diameter and had 5 inches removed in the center, leaving 2½ inches of fabric for the length of the flounce.)

7 Pin the flounce to the sleeve extension, right sides together. Stitch using a ½-inch seam allowance, and trim away any excess flounce. Press the flounce out. Repeat for the second flounce.

8 Fold the sleeve extension in half, right sides together, lining up the seam, and pin. Sew using a ½-inch seam allowance. Using a zigzag stitch or serger, finish the raw edge of the ruffled cuff as desired.

9 Turn the shirt inside out. Pin the wrong side of the sleeve extension to the wrong side of the existing sleeve, placing the edge of the ruffled cuff ½ inch above the edge of the existing sleeve. Stitch using a narrow seam allowance. Turn the shirt right side out.

10 If you will use purchased bias binding for the collar, skip step 10. If you want to make your own continuous bias strips for binding the edges, use these instructions. To make bias strips, begin by cutting a rectangle of silk fabric along the straight grain; fold one corner so the edges meet (figure 2). Press and open; the pressed fold is the true bias. Use this crease to begin marking strips of the appropriate width (2½ inches in this project) and cut away the excess (figure 3). Place the right sides together, matching the marked lines, and stitch in a narrow seam, with one strip extending on either side; cut along the lines (figure 4). Fold in half and press.

Figure 1

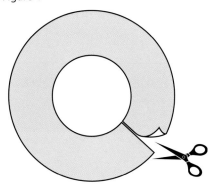

Figure 2

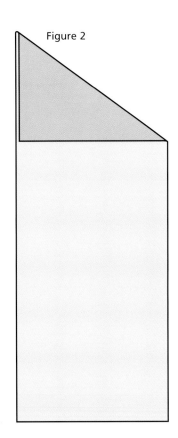

Figure 3

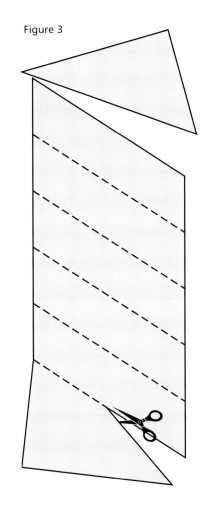

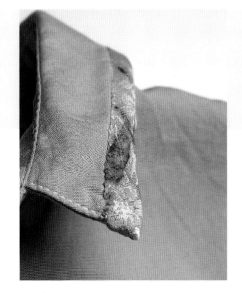

11 Trim the collar to about 1¼ inches long. Beginning at one end of the collar, pin the bias binding or tape to the raw edge, right sides together. Leave an extra ½ inch at either end. Stitch and trim the seam. Fold the binding over the seam to the wrong side and hand stitch in place, folding under the ends.

12 To create the fabric flower, cut at least four 5-inch-diameter circles out of the scrap cuff and/or binding fabric. Finish off the edges by zigzag stitching or serging.

13 Layer the fabric circles and then fold the entire stack into quarters (in half, then in half again at the center). Hand stitch through all the layers at the center point, and then knot securely. Using a small safety pin, pin the flower to the shirt as you wish.

✳ Note

This designer has experience with surface design, and thus she used fabric that she had dyed for the sleeve extensions and the self-made bias binding. She also added some decorative stitching to the fabric. And, she dyed the shirt to match before she began the project. If these skills aren't in your repertoire, you can easily imitate this look by using purchased fabrics and binding. Start with the blouse color and then shop for complementary fabric and embellishments.

Figure 4

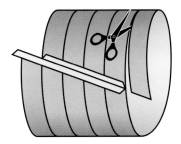

Appliquéd Pants

Use a creative appliqué technique to embellish these nondescript pants.

Choose a complementary print fabric and some sharp buttons to create this look.

Embellished by Jessica Kemp

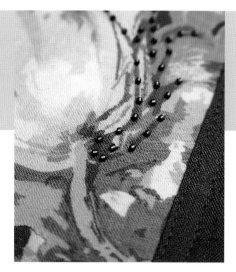

Materials & Tools

Linen/cotton pants

Print fabric to complement pants, approximately ½ yard

Paper-backed fusible web, approximately ½ yard

Beading thread

1 tube of seed beads to complement the pants

Buttons to complement the pants (optional)

Seam ripper

Scissors

Beading needle

Sewing machine

Tape measure

Iron

Dressmaker's pins

Instructions

1 Use a seam ripper to tear out the seam on one pant leg.

2 Build a fabric appliqué by cutting out elements of the printed fabric and applying them to the pant leg. Use the fusible web to bond the elements in place, following the manufacturer's instructions.

3 Using a beading needle and beading thread, embellish the area with single-stitch beading as desired. (See Beading Techniques on page 122.) Sew the seam back together.

4 Measure the waistband and cut a piece of fabric to these dimensions, adding ⅝ inch to the width. Turn under ½ inch along the long bottom edge of the fabric piece and press. Pin the right side of the fabric piece along the inside of the waistband and stitch using a narrow ⅛-inch seam allowance. Turn the fabric to the outside and then stitch to the waistband along the pressed edge.

5 Add fabric appliqués to the center of the waistband as described in step 2.

6 If desired, replace the buttons on the waistband and back pockets.

White Flower Skirt

Transform a dowdy, but good quality, wool skirt into something considerably more flirty, using felted remnants, a bit of crewel wool, and some tiny shirt buttons.

Embellished by Terry Taylor

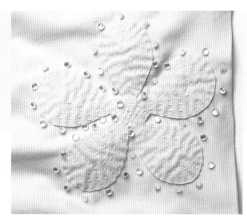

Materials & Tools

Wool skirt

Thread to match the skirt

Roll of fusible bonding web

1 skein of three-strand crewel wool

48 buttons, each approximately ⅜ inch wide

Tape measure

Dressmaker's pencil

Scissors

Dressmaker's pins

Sewing machine

Needles (one sewing needle and one crewel needle)

Instructions

1 Shorten the skirt to the desired length, measuring and marking as needed. Hem the skirt (or use fusible bonding web).

2 Felt the wool you cut off the skirt in step 1 by washing it in warm water. To make sure that it felts thoroughly, you can toss the wool piece into the dryer with a non-pilling item. Dry on high heat. (Read about felting on page 15.)

3 Draw a bold floral shape on the felted wool. Cut it out.

4 Fuse the floral shape onto the skirt using the fusible bonding web, following the manufacturer's instructions.

5 Thread the crewel needle with one strand of crewel wool. Outline the shape using a bold running stitch and fill in each petal as desired. Use a cross-stitch or other decorative stitch to accent the center of the flower. (See Embroidery Techniques on page 124.)

6 Sew the buttons around the floral shape, spacing them evenly around the appliqué.

✳ Note

Look for a longish skirt for this project, so you have enough wool remnants to make your appliqué.

✳ Variation

If you prefer a deconstructed look, simply use pinking shears to shorten the skirt in step 1 and do not hem the skirt. You can also use pinking shears to cut the appliqué in step 3.

Sparkling Blue Jeans

The sparkle on these jeans comes from a contemporary application of crewelwork.

Embellished by Katherine Shaughnessy

Materials & Tools

Blue jeans

Crewel wool in two complementary colors, 1 skein each

Water-soluble marking pen

Embroidery hoop, 5 inches or smaller

Size 24 chenille needle (or comparable size)

Figure 1

Instructions

1 Draw a sprinkling of dots randomly along the bottom edge of each pant leg, making sure to go all the way around each leg. You may wish to elaborate on each dot by drawing out multiple lines from the center circle. Place a portion of one pant leg in the hoop.

2 Make a knot in the end of your thread. (Unlike traditional crewel done on linen, this project requires that you make a new knot in the end of your thread before beginning each motif.)

3 Embroider the sparkles starting from the center of your design and working out, using a straight stitch to make "spokes" that share a center point. Always stitch *down* through the same center point and come *up* at the edges. (See figure 1; for more information, see Embroidery Techniques on page 124.)

4 Make sure to make a knot at the completion of each motif. (In case one of the sparkles wears out over time and the thread breaks, you will only lose one sparkle instead of all of them.) Alternate between the two colors as you work and vary the size of each sparkle.

5 Reposition the hoop as necessary until you have embroidered all the way around each pant leg.

✳ Note

Give each leg a quick press with a warm iron if you prefer. However, since wool has been added to these cotton jeans, they should be washed in cold water and hung to dry. Wool will shrink in warm water or in a hot dryer.

Tiered Skirt with Attached Shawl

A variegated shawl becomes the perfect accessory *and* embellishment for this tiered skirt. The gleam of the rayon shawl offers just the right complement to the cotton skirt.

Embellished by Jessica Kemp

Materials & Tools

Tiered cotton skirt

Variegated shawl to complement the skirt

Thread to match the shawl

Scissors

Tape measure

Iron

Dressmaker's pins

Sewing machine

Needle

Instructions

1 Cut away the bottom tier of the skirt to insert piping made from the shawl. Begin by measuring the circumference of the skirt where the bottom tier was stitched in place. Add ½ inch to this measurement and cut a strip of the shawl to this length by 1 inch wide. (Be sure to save the fringe from the scarf to use in step 2.) Fold the strip in half lengthwise, press, and pin it ¼ inch under the skirt where the tier was removed, turning under the raw edge of one end and overlapping the other end where the strips meet. Baste in place.

2 Add the fringe from the shawl to the hem of the tier you cut away in step 1. Measure and cut the fringe to the circumference of the skirt plus 1 inch to turn under the raw edges. Press under the raw edges, and then stitch in place. Pin the fringe to the wrong side of the hem and stitch in place. (This skirt originally had a lace trim at the hem that was cut away before the fringe was added).

3 Pin the removed tier under the piping you made from the shawl in step 1 and stitch the skirt back together, following the initial stitching line. (Make sure that the raw edge of the removed tier is just beyond the stitching line before you begin to sew.)

4 Take the remainder of the shawl fabric and stitch it to the top edge of the waistband. Gather the shawl at the right side of the waist and tack in place as you wish. Tie the shawl at the left side.

Beaded Gauntlets

These festive gauntlets have the appropriate mixture of fancy and folly for a special night out.

Embellished by Dana Irwin

Materials & Tools

Acrylic knit gloves

1-inch-wide beaded trim, approximately ½ yard

¼-inch-wide velvet trim, approximately ½ yard

Thread to match the gloves

Scissors

Crochet hook, 3 mm (size D U.S.)

Dressmaker's pins

Needles (one sewing needle and one tapestry needle)

Instructions

1 Trim the fingers and thumbs off the gloves, cutting the gloves evenly four knitted rows above the desired length. Unravel the yarn to this spot without cutting the yarn.

2 Using the crochet hook, slip stitch through the row of looped stitches using the length of the unraveled yarn. (See figures 1 and 2; for more information, see Crochet Techniques on page 121.) Repeat for the thumb. Weave in the ends.

3 Pin the beaded trim in place around the finger openings. Sew it to the gauntlets using a small running stitch. Whipstitch the velvet trim on top, being sure to cover up the row of running stitches. Repeat this step to decorate the thumb openings.

✳ Note

Fabric or leather gloves can also be used to make a similar project. After you cut the fabric gloves, turn them inside out, make a narrow hem, and secure the seams with whipstitches. There's no need to hem the leather gloves, but do secure the seams as for the fabric gloves.

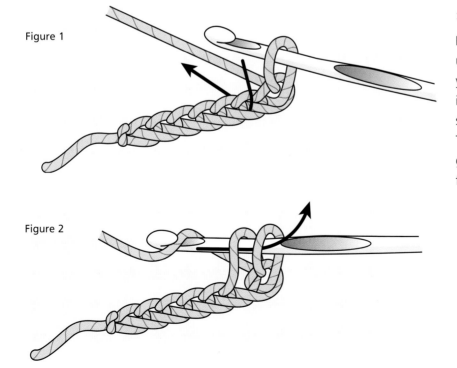

Figure 1

Figure 2

Pants with Woven Ribbons

Smart two-sided ribbon is woven through the shiny eyelets on these pants. A regular pair of pants is now ready for a night of dancing.

Embellished by Rain Newcomb

Materials & Tools

Cotton pants

Thread to match the pants

Fusible interfacing, approximately 1 yard

½-inch-wide silver eyelets, 2 packages

⅜-inch-wide two-sided ribbon, about 4 feet for each pant leg

Dressmaker's pins

Tape measure

Seam ripper

Newspaper

Liquid seam sealant

Needle

Iron

Water-soluble marking pen

Craft knife

Eyelet setter

Hammer

Instructions

1 Try on the pants and decide on the length of the ribbon embellishment. (On this pair, it ends about 2 inches above the knee.) Stick a pin in the seam of the pants at that point. Measure this length and mark the other leg with a pin as well.

2 Using the seam ripper, open up the seam to the marked spot. (Before you start ripping, make sure you're taking out the seam on the outside of the pants, not the inside!) Repeat on the other pant leg.

3 Turn the pants inside out and place them on the newspaper. Apply the liquid seam sealant to the raw edge, following the manufacturer's instructions. Let it dry.

4 Thread the needle and reinforce the top of the seam with extra stitches. Turn the pants right side out.

5 Make a 3-inch-deep fold at the cuff, tucking the extra fabric to the inside of the pants.

6 Pinching at the fold, hold the cuff in one hand and the top of the open seam in the other hand. Pull the fabric taut and it will fold from cuff to end. Pin the fold in place. Press the fold.

7 Repeat steps 5 and 6 on the other open edges.

8 Cut four pieces of fusible interfacing, each 2 inches wide and as long as the opening in the pants. Tuck the interfacing into the fold and press according to the manufacturer's instructions. Repeat for the other three open edges. (The interfacing helps reinforce the fabric when you set the eyelets.)

9 To mark the placement of the eyelets, measure 1 inch from the top of the opening and mark. Mark every 2 inches along the opening; repeat along each opened seam. (If you'd like the eyelets in the pants to be diagonal from each other, measure 2 inches down from the opening on the opposing side and mark every 2 inches after that.)

10 Set the eyelets using the craft knife, eyelet setter, and hammer, following the setter's instructions. Apply liquid seam sealant to the raw edges if desired.

11 Apply liquid seam sealant to both ends of the two pieces of ribbon and let it dry. Lace the ribbon through the eyelets on each leg, adjusting the length as you wish.

Cardigan with Felt Appliqués

If you've ever lost a favorite sweater to an unplanned trip through the washing machine, here's a way to save it. Let it be reborn as a cardigan with jazzy mid-century accents.

Embellished by Jen Swearington

Materials & Tools

Felted wool crewneck sweater

Bias tape to complement the sweater, approximately 1 yard

Thread to match the bias tape

Snap tape, approximately ½ yard

Thread to match the sweater

Scrap felt pieces in various colors

Thread to match the felt

Scissors

Dressmaker's pins

Sewing machine

Iron and ironing board

Instructions

1 Begin with a wool sweater that has been felted by washing in the washing machine; it will shrink during this process, so plan accordingly. (A synthetic sweater will not felt, so make sure the sweater is wool. Read about felting on page 15.) Cut off one sleeve at an angle so it forms a point at the bend in the arm. To make sure they're the same size and shape, use the removed sleeve as a template for cutting the remaining sleeve.

2 Beginning at the point of the sleeve, encase the raw edge with the bias tape, pinning as you go. Leave an extra ½ inch of bias tape at the end, fold under the raw edge, and overlap the other end. Using thread that matches the bias tape, stitch the bias tape onto the sleeve.

3 Cut straight up the middle of the sweater, being careful not to cut into the back.

4 Separate the two halves of the snap tape. Pin one strip of snap tape to the right side of the sweater, right sides together. Cut the snap tape so it lines up with the bottom of the sweater.

5 Using thread that matches the sweater, sew along the neckline, center opening, and bottom edge using a narrow seam allowance. Turn the snap tape to the inside, press, and pin in place. Topstitch along the edge of the snap tape to secure.

6 To stretch the left side of the sweater and form the asymmetrical opening, sew along the raw edge with a zigzag stitch or serger, pulling gently as you go. Fold the raw edge to the inside about ¼ inch. Press into place and pin, then topstitch.

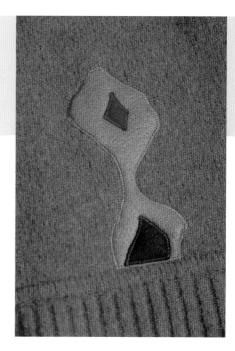

7 Pin the other strip of snap tape, right side up, to the edge of the stretched opening. Make sure the snaps line up with those on the other side. Tuck under the raw edges at the top and bottom and pin in place. Topstitch all the way around the tape to secure it.

8 Cut out some fun felt shapes and pin them onto the sweater as desired. Using a narrow zigzag stitch and thread that matches the felt, stitch completely around the outside edge of the shapes, attaching them securely to the sweater.

Embroidered Cropped Pants

Nothing suits a spring afternoon better than these bright green pants with rows of botanically inspired machine embroidery.

Embellished by Kelledy Francis

Materials & Tools

Polyester/rayon pants

Tear-away stabilizer

Machine embroidery thread in a contrasting color

Thread to match the pants

Seam ripper

Dressmaker's pins

Dressmaker's pencil

Sewing machine

Machine embroidery needle

Embroidery presser foot (if required)

Instructions

1 Use a seam ripper to open up the seam on one side of each pant leg, being sure to remove enough stitching so that the pant leg will lie flat when you embroider the pants.

2 Pin the tear-away stabilizer to the wrong side of each pant leg.

3 Use a dressmaker's pencil to mark the location for the lines of embroidery. Make a pattern comprising three different stitches and add to each pant leg. When you have completed the embroidery, remove the excess stabilizer, following the manufacturer's instructions. Using thread that matches the pants, sew the leg seams together again.

4 If your pants feature pocket flaps, decorate them with machine embroidery as well.

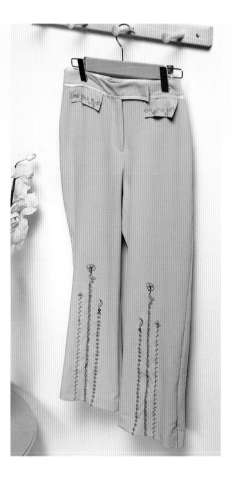

✳ Note

If your sewing machine doesn't offer many embroidery stitches, you can achieve this look by combining rows of straight and zigzag stitches, varying the widths and lengths to create a graphic design. You can also use a variety of hand embroidery stitches to capture the botanical feel of this project.

Bejeweled Skirt

An unadorned skirt with a flattering cut becomes a memorable garment when it's decorated with shimmering bead embroidery.

Embellished by Rain Newcomb

Materials & Tools

Polyester satin skirt with godets

Nylon beading thread, size D

Thread conditioner or beeswax (optional)

Clear nail polish (optional)

40 crystal cubes, 4mm each

1 tube of crystal seed beads, size 8/o

2 tubes of crystal seed beads, size 11/o

2 strands of crystal tear drops, size 8/o

Beading needle, size 12

Scissors

Instructions

1 Thread the beading needle with 1 yard of beading thread. Wax the thread if necessary. Double the thread and tie a double knot in the end.

2 Begin on the back of the skirt to perfect your technique before you work on the front. Knot to anchor the thread on the wrong side of the skirt, about ¼ inch above the point of the godet. You will lay the line of the beadwork along the seamline of the godet as you work. If you wish, dab a bit of the clear nail polish on the knot. This will cement the thread, making the knot stronger.

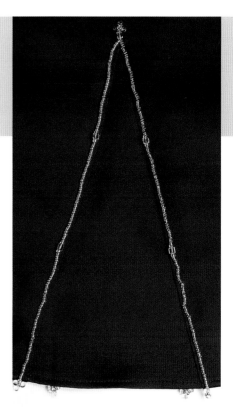

3 Put one size 8/o seed bead, one 4mm cube, and one 8/o seed bead on the thread. Sew through the skirt, anchoring the beads in place. Come back through the cloth at the beginning of the bead sequence and pass through all three beads.

4 Add five 11/o seed beads to the thread. Sew through the skirt, anchoring them in place. Backstitch so the needle comes out between the second and third seed bead. Pass through the last three seed beads (figure 1).

5 Repeat step 4, following the seamline on the godet until you've sewed 3 inches of beads in place. (You may need to adjust this figure based on the length of your skirt.)

6 Thread an 8/o seed bead, a 4mm cube, and an 8/o seed bead into place as you did in step 3.

7 Sew another 3 inches of 11/o seed beads into place. Repeat step 6 and sew 3 more inches of seed beads into place.

8 When you reach the hem of the skirt, anchor the last beads you added. Then add three more 11/o seed beads and an 8/o seed bead. Do not anchor these beads to the fabric.

9 Add three tear drops to the thread. Push all the beads up so that there are no gaps in the thread. Send the needle back through all three teardrops, forming a loop (see figure 2).

10 Pass through the 8/o and three 11/o seed beads. Thread the needle through the line of beadwork all the way to the top of the godet. This will help straighten the beadwork.

11 At the top of the godet, exit through the 4mm cube and 8/o seed beads. Add three tear drops and form another loop as you did in step 9.

12 Go back through the 8/o seed bead, the 4mm cube, and the 8/o seed bead. Then repeat steps 4 through 10 on the other side of the godet.

13 Repeat steps 1 through 12 to embroider along each godet on the skirt.

✳ Note

If you use crystal beads, choose a color of beading thread one shade lighter than the color of the fabric to give this project an elegant look. For more flair, pick a fun color that contrasts with the color of the skirt.

For additional information, see Beading Techniques on page 122.

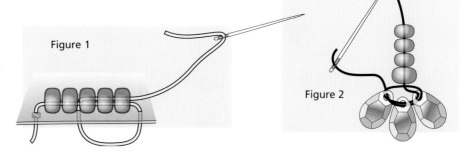

Figure 1

Figure 2

Skirt with Silk Appliqués

Gleaming silk appliqués bring dimension and life to this basic
wraparound skirt. Metallic sequins complete the exotic transformation.

Embellished by Joan K. Morris

Materials & Tools

Wool wraparound skirt

Paper for pattern

Paper-backed fusible web

Dupioni silk, approximately
1 yard in one color and
approximately ½ yard in a
complementary color

Pencil

Thread that matches each color
of silk

Heart-shaped sequins (optional)

Ruler

Scissors (one pair craft and one
pair fabric)

Iron

Dressmaker's pins

Sewing machine

Tape measure

Needle

Seam ripper or craft knife

Instructions

1 Create paper patterns for your silk appliqués, beginning with the edging. It's easiest to do this if you first trace the shape of the skirt onto the paper and then draw your design onto the paper template. Cut out the edging pattern with craft scissors.

2 Place the edging pattern on the fusible web and cut it out, following the manufacturer's instructions about the proper orientation of elements. (You may need to piece the edging together to fit the circumference of the skirt.) Iron the pieces cut from the fusible web onto the wrong side of the yard of silk as directed by the manufacturer of the fusible web.

3 Include an extra ½ inch all the way around as you cut each fused piece from the silk, using fabric scissors. Use this quilter's trick to finish the edges: After you remove the paper backing on the fusible web, fold under the extra ½ inch of fabric and use an iron to press it carefully into the bonding material. Do *not* let the iron touch the fusible web. (When you apply the appliqués to the skirt, this ½-inch area will not bond to the skirt, of course, but will be topstitched into place.)

4 Remove any buttons from the skirt. Open the skirt and press the edging into place per the manufacturer's instructions, covering the buttonhole. Pin as necessary. Stitch close to each edge with matching thread.

5 Make a paper pattern for the triangles, in whatever size you like. (These are 6 inches wide at the base and 3 inches tall.)

6 Measure around the skirt and decide how many triangles you want in each color of silk. (Remember that the front of the skirt will overlap.) Use the paper patterns to cut out the fusible web and follow the manufacturer's instructions to adhere the pieces cut from the fusible web to the appropriate color of silk. Cut the triangles from the silk, adding the additional ½ inch as in step 3. Trim the fabric at each

corner to ¼ inch. Carefully press each point at the corners first, then press under the edges as in step 3.

7 Starting at the front along the bottom edging, press all the triangles onto the skirt per the manufacturer's instructions. Slightly overlap the base of the triangles at the seam line of the edging.

8 Stitch the triangles in place; it may be easiest to stitch all the way along the bottom of the triangles first.

9 To remake a buttonhole, work from the wrong side of the skirt and zigzag over the old buttonhole with short narrow stitches. Use a seam ripper or craft knife to slash the new buttonhole from the right side. Replace the button. If you wish, sew the sequins on the skirt to accent the triangles.

Deconstructed Sweater with Lace

Alter a boring sweater and give it a vintage look with a bit of lace, contrasting yarn, and a dramatic velvet rose—complete with feather.

Embellished by Jen Swearington

Materials & Tools

Wool crewneck sweater

Thread to match the sweater

3½-inch-wide lace, approximately 1½ yards

Thick chenille yarn in a contrasting color, approximately 3 yards

Thread to match the lace

2 hook-and-eye closures

Fabric rose

Scissors

Tape measure

Dressmaker's pins

Sewing machine

Iron

Needle

Instructions

1. Cut off the sleeves to elbow length. After cutting off the first sleeve, use it as a template to make sure the other sleeve is the same length.

2. Cut a 2-inch slit down the front center of the collar, as well as a 1-inch slit into the shoulder seams (from the collar). Fold under along the cuts (including the neckband) and pin.

Topstitch ½ inch away from the neckline. Trim off the excess fabric.

3 Beginning at the end of the right sleeve, fold ½ inch of the lace around the edge of the sleeve and pin. Run the lace from the end of the sleeve, across the shoulder and neckline, and down the back of sweater. Fold the edge of the lace around the hem of the sweater as you did at the sleeve. Cut away the excess lace at the hem. Carefully pin the lace in place, making sure it lies flat.

4 Place the yarn next to one edge of the lace and couch the yarn onto the lace while stitching the lace onto the sweater, using thread that matches the lace. (A whipstitch will work, too.) Continue stitching the yarn onto the lace when it is in between the two sides of the sweater. When the lace reaches the sweater again, stitch back into it as before. Continue to the end of the lace and repeat along the opposite edge of the lace.

5 Measure the circumference of the sleeve, add 1 inch, and cut a piece of lace this length for the cuff. Sew the ends of the lace together, right sides facing, using a ½-inch seam allowance

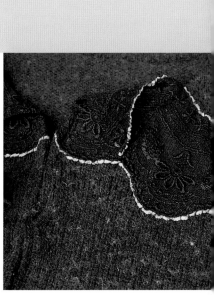

6 With right sides together, pin the cuff to the sleeve and machine stitch, using a narrow seam allowance.

7 Using a zigzag stitch or serger, finish the cuff seam allowance of the wool sweater to keep it from unraveling. Finish the raw edge only after attaching the lace or you will stretch out the sleeve.

8 Apply the yarn along the seam between the cuff and the sweater, using the method described in step 4.

9 Cut straight up the middle of the front of the sweater and through the lace. Trim the sides of the sweater into gentle curves ending at the side seams, being careful not to cut into the back.

10 Narrowly fold under the raw edges of the lace, yarn, and sweater, press, and pin. Topstitch the lace along the folded edges, including the lace. Topstitch the lace to the neckline. Allow the lace extension at the neck edge to fall open, creating an asymmetrical collar, as shown above.

11 Sew two hook-and-eye closures along the front of the sweater.

12 Attach the rose pin as you wish.

Tailored Jacket with Applied Fabric

Graphic fabric appliqués impart a bold look
to this unassuming white jacket.

Embellished by Joan K. Morris

Materials & Tools

Cotton twill jacket

Paper for making patterns

Paper-backed fusible web,
approximately 2 yards

2 patterned fabrics in complementary colors, approximately
½ yard each

Piping to complement the fabric,
approximately 5 yards

Thread to match each fabric

Roll of fusible bonding web

Felt in a complementary color,
approximately ½ yard

1 button, approximately
1 inch wide (optional)

2 buttons, each approximately
¾ inch wide (optional)

Pencil

Scissors (one pair craft and one
pair fabric)

Dressmaker's pins

Iron

Sewing machine

Seam ripper or craft knife

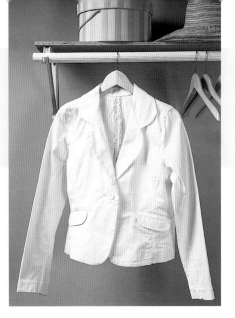

Instructions

1 Create paper patterns for each section you plan to decorate; you will transfer these patterns to the paper-backed fusible web to make each appliqué. Open the jacket so one side is as flat as possible. Place the paper over the flat side of the jacket, trace over the appropriate section, and cut it out with craft scissors. Place the pattern on the jacket and alter it to fit as needed. Make all necessary pieces in this fashion.

2 Place the paper pattern pieces on the fusible web and cut new pieces from the bonding material, following the manufacturer's instructions about the proper orientation of elements.

3 Begin by making the appliqués for the center front *only*. Fold one of the pieces of fabric right sides together. Pin the paper patterns to the fabric. With fabric scissors, cut out the fabric pieces, adding an extra ½ inch all the way around each piece.

4 Following the manufacturer's instructions, apply each fusible piece to its matching fabric piece, and then use this quilter's trick to finish the edges: After you remove the paper backing on the fusible web, fold under the extra ½ inch of fabric and carefully press it into the bonding material. Do *not* let the iron touch the fusible web. (When you apply the appliqués to the jacket, this ½-inch area will not bond to the jacket, of course, but will be topstitched into place.)

5 Remove any buttons from the jacket. Press the appliqués onto the jacket per the manufacturer's instructions, covering any buttonholes.

6 Now you will topstitch around the first set of appliqués and add the piping. Slide the piping under the fabric pieces, hiding the ends of the trim by pushing them under the fabric. Topstitch as close to the edge as you can.

7 Repeat steps 3 through 6 to apply appliqués at the side of the jacket, using the remaining fabric.

8 Use the same fabric for the appliqués on the arms as well. Apply the paper-backed fusible web as described in steps 3 through 5, but since it is impossible to top-stitch the appliqués along the length of the arms, stitch the pieces in place at either end—the wrist and the underarm seam. Cut pieces from the roll of bonding web to adhere the edges of the arm pieces to the jacket. Follow the manufacturer's instructions to apply.

9 For the collar and pockets, use felt and paper-backed fusible web to make the appliqués, as described in steps 3 through 6. Because felt doesn't ravel, you don't need to add the extra ½-inch to the felt pieces.

10 To remake a buttonhole, work from the wrong side of the jacket and zigzag over the old buttonhole with short narrow stitches. Use a seam ripper or craft knife to slash the new buttonhole from the right side. Replace the buttons, if desired.

✳ Note

Because of the various fabrics used in this project, including dark felt, it is probably best to dry-clean this jacket.

Illustrated Techniques & Glossary

This guide will introduce you to all of the techniques used in *Exquisite Embellishments for Your Clothes*. A glossary of terms follows the illustrated guide to the various techniques.

Sewing Techniques

Some of the stitches in this section and the embroidery section are interchangeable, as they can be used in dressmaking or embroidery.

Belt carrier. A series of thread loops covered with blanket or buttonhole stitches (figure 1). Also called a thread bar.

Blanket stitch. This loop stitch can be decorative or functional. After knotting and anchoring the thread near the fabric edge from the wrong side, insert the needle from the right side so it's perpendicular to the fabric edge. Pass the needle over the thread and pull. Pass the needle over the thread with each successive stitch (figure 2).

Buttonhole stitch. Buttonhole stitch is similar to blanket stitch, but forms a knot at the fabric edge. Working with the needle perpendicular to the fabric edge and the thread behind the needle, loop the thread around the needle and pull (figure 3).

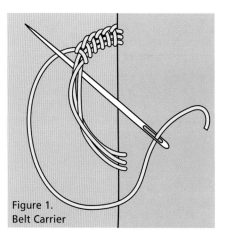

Figure 1.
Belt Carrier

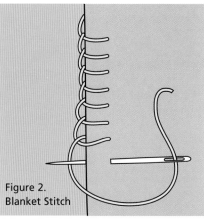

Figure 2.
Blanket Stitch

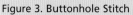
Figure 3. Buttonhole Stitch

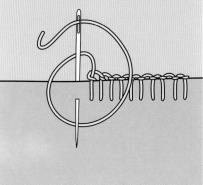

Satin stitch. In machine stitching, make a satin stitch with a zigzag stitch set to a short length, so the stitches are very close together. For hand stitching, see the Embroidery Stitches section on page 124.

Topstitch. Machine stitching on the right side of the garment that follows an edge or a seam.

Whipstitch. A utilitarian slanted hand stitch where the needle is inserted perpendicular to the fabric edge (figure 4).

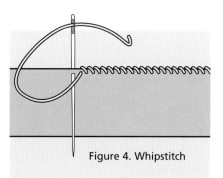

Figure 4. Whipstitch

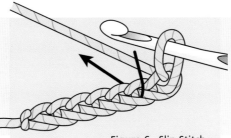

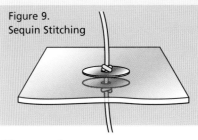
Figure 9.
Sequin Stitching

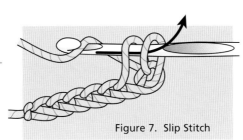
Figure 6. Slip Stitch

Crochet Techniques

The crochet stitches used in this book are simple and easy to learn. A hook, some yarn, a pair of scissors, and a yarn needle will get you started.

Chain. In traditional crocheting, you would first make a slip knot and begin to work by making a foundation of chain stitches. In this book, the chain stitches are created by working into a row of whipstitches along the edge of a garment, but the technique is the same. Use the crochet hook to pull up a short loop of yarn through one of the whip-stitches, leaving a loose tail that is several inches long. Insert the hook down into the next whipstitch. Catch the yarn from the skein with the hook. Use the hook to pull up the yarn through the whipstitch and the first loop (figure 5). Continue by inserting the hook into the next whipstitch; repeat as needed.

Figure 7. Slip Stitch

Slip stitch. In another departure from traditional crocheting, the slip stitches used here are worked into a row of existing knitting but again, the techniques are the same. Insert the hook into the second chain from the hook (figure 6), wrap the yarn over the hook and pull through both stitches (figure 7). You will have one loop left on the hook; repeat as needed.

Weave in ends. To weave in any loose ends, thread an end through the yarn needle and pass through the last loop of your work. Weave the tail back and forth through the crochet work for about 2 inches, locking the yarn in place. Do not knot the yarn ends.

Sequin Techniques

There are several different ways to attach sequins to your embellished garments.

If you prefer to hide the thread, add a bead in the center of the sequin. Stitch through the center of the bead from the wrong side, add the bead, and stitch down through the center (figure 8).

If you'd like for the thread to be part of the embellishment, stitch down through the center of the sequin, leaving the knot and tail visible. Add a sequin on the other side of the fabric and knot (figure 9). This technique is well suited for use on scarves or any item where both sides are easily seen.

If you'd like to add a line of sequins, use backstitches to secure the sequins (figure 10). This technique is very similar to the bead technique described on page 122.

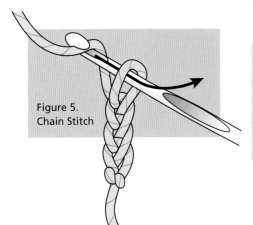
Figure 5.
Chain Stitch

Figure 8. Sequin Stitching

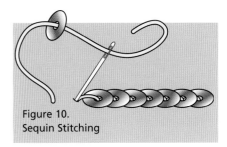
Figure 10.
Sequin Stitching

Beading Techniques

Simple bead embroidery can add dazzling highlights to any purchased garment. To begin, you need only thread, a needle, and, of course, beads. There are specialized threads and needles for beading, but many of the projects in this book use clear nylon thread that you find among sewing notions. Any fine needle that will pass through the beads can be used as well. Use your local bead shop as a resource when planning a beading project.

Make a sketch of your design before you begin, and make a sample on your garment to confirm bead color and thread choice. If your garment allows, use an embroidery hoop to stabilize the fabric and prevent puckering while you work.

Tension is important in bead embroidery, but it's better to work too loosely than too tightly. If you have really noticeable gaps in the thread, you can add a bead. Although your line of beading may be imperfect at close inspection, the lines magically straighten when you move some distance away!

Finally, note that if you put beads on an area of a garment that will get a lot of wear, you may compromise the longevity of your work; if the glass beads break they may cut into the thread. And once the thread is cut, all the beads you painstakingly added will likely be lost.

Here are four techniques used in *Exquisite Embellishments for Your Clothes*.

Single stitch. This is basically a running stitch with a bead in each stitch. Each time the needle emerges from the wrong side of the fabric, slide a bead onto it and down to the fabric. Push the needle through to the wrong side just at the edge of the bead (figure 11).

Backstitch. Add an uninterrupted line of beads using the backstitch, attaching either single beads or groups of beads. This stitch is similar to backstitch in regular sewing, with a bead added. To add a single bead, slide a bead onto the needle each time it emerges from the fabric and insert the needle at the edge of the previous bead. Begin the next stitch one bead's length away (figure 12).

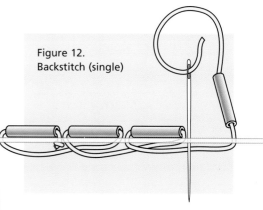

Figure 12.
Backstitch (single)

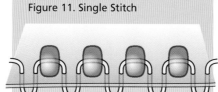

Figure 11. Single Stitch

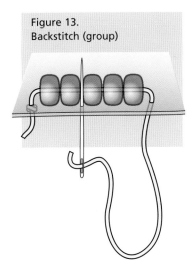

Figure 13.
Backstitch (group)

To backstitch groups of beads, slide five beads onto the thread and stitch into the fabric. Backstitch so the needle emerges between the second and third bead (figure 13). Pass the needle through these beads (figure 14) and then add the next group of five beads, continuing in this fashion until the line of beading is complete.

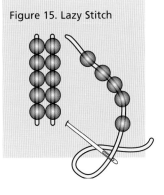

Figure 15. Lazy Stitch

Lazy stitch. If you want to add a small line of beads with no stitching in between, use this method. With the needle emerging from the wrong side of the fabric, slide five or six beads onto it and push them to the fabric. Hold them in place as you push the needle back into the fabric just at the edge of the last bead. You can use these lines of beads in geometric patterns or as parts of a motif (figure 15).

Couching. An embroidery technique called couching can be used to hold long lines of beads in place. For single-needle couching, string as many beads as desired to make a line and anchor the string of beads into the fabric. Come up between every few beads and stitch over the beading thread, tacking the line of beads to the fabric (figure 16). Continue for the length of the string of beads; you can make straight or curved lines using this technique.

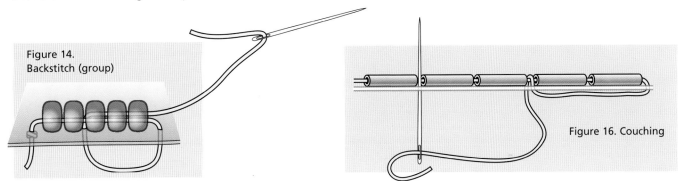

Figure 14.
Backstitch (group)

Figure 16. Couching

Embroidery Techniques

Embroidery is an age-old embellishment technique. The tools and supplies you need for hand embroidery are few: floss, needles, an embroidery hoop, and perhaps a marking tool or quilter's tape. Usually, you will want to separate the floss so you are working with three or fewer strands. Carefully place the garment into the embroidery hoop for stability; mark the placement of your stitches, if necessary.

Here are some basic embroidery stitches, including those used in *Exquisite Embellishments for Your Clothes*.

Running stitch. An easy stitch to execute, the running stitch is simply made by weaving the needle through the garment at evenly spaced intervals (figure 17).

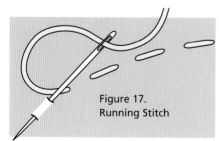

Figure 17.
Running Stitch

Straight stitch. Use a series of straight stitches used to create a motif (figure 18).

Satin stitch. Satin stitch is composed of parallel rows of straight stitches (figure 19).

Cross-stitch. Cross-stitch is a series of diagonal stitches. The finished stitches can be touching one another or separated by space, as desired (figure 20).

French knots. The elegant French knot is created by wrapping the thread around the needle once or twice, then inserting it back into the garment at the point where the needle emerged (figure 21).

Woven wheels. This fanciful stitch can be varied to be as full as desired. Begin by making an odd number of straight stitches and covering them with floss, alternately going over one stitch and under the next (figure 22). You can completely cover the stitches, if desired.

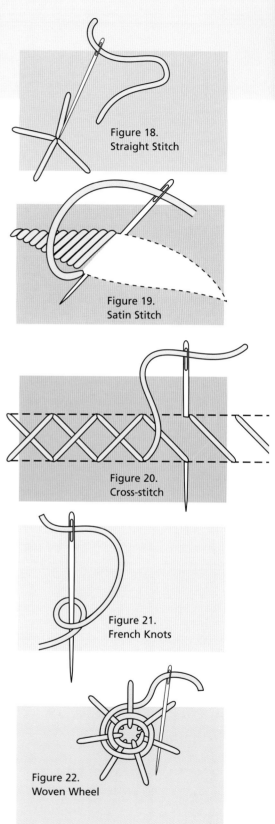

Figure 18.
Straight Stitch

Figure 19.
Satin Stitch

Figure 20.
Cross-stitch

Figure 21.
French Knots

Figure 22.
Woven Wheel

Glossary

Appliqué. The applying of one fabric layer to another.

Baste. Temporary stitching to hold layers in place; can be done by hand or by machine.

Bateau. The "boat" neckline that is wide and shallow.

Bodice. Section of a garment between the shoulder and the waist.

Clip. Snip into the seam allowance to allow ease, usually in a curved seam.

Felting. Melding the fibers of a wool garment by washing and drying.

Flounce. A ruffle that is cut in a circle; flounces are not usually gathered at the stitched edge.

Godet. An inset (generally triangular) to a hemline that adds fullness.

Grosgrain. Ribbon (or fabric) with ribs.

Hem. Finished bottom edge of a garment or a part of a garment (i.e., a sleeve). A narrow hem is created by turning under the raw edge and pressing, then folding under the raw edge to the pressed edge and stitching in place.

Macramé. Technique of knotting material to produce a pattern.

Organza. Fabric that is crisp and lightweight; made of natural or synthetic fibers.

Passementerie. Decorative patterns created with trim.

Pivot. To change direction as you sew by lifting the presser foot and turning the fabric.

Ruching. A form of gathering that can produce a variety of effects.

Ruffle. A strip of gathered fabric. A single ruffle is gathered along one long edge, while a double ruffle (or ruche) is gathered between its two long edges.

Selvage. The finished edge of fabric.

Sheath. Form-fitting dress constructed with a bodice and a straight skirt.

Surplice. Bodice featuring a neckline where one side crosses over the other side.

Tuck. Stitched folds in fabric.

Yoke. A fitted area of a garment; it supports the rest of the garment that is attached to it.

Metric Conversion Chart

Inches	Millimeters (mm)/ Centimeters (cm)
1/8	3 mm
3/16	5 mm
1/4	6 mm
5/16	8 mm
3/8	9.5 mm
7/16	1.1 cm
1/2	1.3 cm
9/16	1.4 cm
5/8	1.6 cm
11/16	1.7 cm
3/4	1.9 cm
13/16	2.1 cm
7/8	2.2 cm
15/16	2.4 cm
1	2.5 cm
1½	3.8 cm
2	5 cm
2½	6.4 cm
3	7.6 cm
3½	8.9 cm
4	10.2 cm
4½	11.4 cm
5	12.7 cm
5½	14 cm
6	15.2 cm
6½	16.5 cm
7	17.8 cm
7½	19 cm
8	20.3 cm

Inches	Millimeters (mm)/ Centimeters (cm)
8½	21.6 cm
9 (¼ yard)	22.9 cm
9½	24.1 cm
10	25.4 cm
10½	26.7 cm
11	27.9 cm
11½	29.2 cm
12	30.5 cm
12½	31.8 cm
13	33 cm
13½	34.3 cm
14	35.6 cm
14½	36.8 cm
15	38.1 cm
15½	39.4 cm
16	40.6 cm
16½	41.9 cm
17	43.2 cm
17½	44.5 cm
18 (½ yard)	45.7 cm
18½	47 cm
19	48.3 cm
19½	49.5 cm
20	50.8 cm
20½	52 cm
21	53.3
21½	54.6
22	55 cm
22½	57.2 cm

Inches	Millimeters (mm)/ Centimeters (cm)
23	58.4 cm
23½	59.7 cm
24	61 cm
24½	62.2 cm
25	63.5 cm
25½	64.8 cm
26	66 cm
26½	67.3 cm
27	68.6 cm
27½	69.9 cm
28	71.1 cm
28½	72.4 cm
29	73.7 cm
29½	74.9 cm
30	76.2 cm
30½	77.5 cm
31	78.7 cm
31½	80 cm
32	81.3 cm
32½	82.6 cm
33	83.8 cm
33½	85 cm
34	86.4 cm
34½	87.6 cm
35	88.9 cm
35½	90.2 cm
36 (1 yard)	91.4 cm

Designer Bios

CAREY BAKER is an Asheville, N.C., native and graduate of the Savannah College of Art and Design. While there, she earned a B.F.A. in fibers, with a focus in computer-aided surface design. Carey enjoys taking a more hands-on approach as well, creating clothing, accessories, home décor, and handmade books. Right now, screenprinting is her major interest; she sells screenprinted, beaded handbags and plans to open a shop in the Asheville area.

STACEY BUDGE is an art director at Lark Books. When she is not designing books, she can be found gardening and knitting at her home in Asheville, N.C.

BROOKE DICKSON is a graduate of the School of Design at North Carolina State University. She studied in the landscape architecture department, as well as in the art and design department. Her interests include collage, paper crafts, gardening, and any chance to be creative! Brooke resides in Asheville, N.C., with her husband, Peter, and son, Jack.

KELLEDY FRANCIS is an artist and seamstress living in Asheville, N.C. She specializes in custom sewing work and outrageous art fashion. She has a B.F.A. from the Maryland Institute, College of Art, where she majored in fiber arts. She is currently pursuing an M.F.A. at Western Carolina University in Cullowhee, N.C. Kelledy also contributed to *Hip Handbags* (Lark Books, 2005) and is looking forward to future sewing and design challenges.

DANA IRWIN is a designer who has been living in embellished clothing all of her adult life. She paints, dances, and sings, and has designed projects, books, and magazines at Lark Books since 1980.

JESSICA KEMP is a Chicago native now living in Asheville, N.C. Her first career was in environmental education, but she now works at Make Me! Fabrics, a vintage and modern fabric store, where she organizes fashion shows and other events. She recently started her own label called Back to Her Place, offering one-of-a-kind embellished thrift-store finds and original designs for both women and men.

MEGAN KIRBY is an art director for Lark Books. She loves fixing up old houses, hunting for antiques, arranging flowers, and designing her own clothes.

MARTHE LE VAN is a jewelry editor for Lark Books and a freelance project designer. Her work has recently been featured in *Hardware Style* (Lark Books, 2003), *Shelf Expression* (Lark Books, 2004), and *The Michaels Book of Paper Crafts* (Lark Books, 2005).

NATHALIE MORNU has made projects for numerous Lark books, including *Decorating Your First Apartment* (2002), *The Weekend Crafter: Making Gingerbread Houses* (2004), and *Hip Handbags* (2005). She lives in Asheville, N.C., but looks for shiny things wherever she may be.

The artistic endeavors of JOAN K. MORRIS have led her down many successful creative paths, including ceramics and costume design for motion pictures. Joan has contributed projects for numerous Lark books, including *Beautiful Ribbon Crafts* (2003), *Halloween: A Grown-up's Guide to Creative Costumes* (2003), *Hardware Style* (2003), *The Michaels Book of Wedding Crafts* (2005), *Hip Handbags* (2005), and many more.

RAIN NEWCOMB enjoys reading children's books, giving her poodle mohawks, and playing with her beads. She also likes things that begin with the letters "C" and "D," words like irrelevant and irreverence, and compound sentences. She lives in Asheville, N.C., and modeled the projects she made for this book (and several others she wishes she had made).

Artist-designer KATHERINE SHAUGHNESSY began sewing crewel embroidery kits at a very young age. She now makes modern crewel embroidery kits through her company, Wool & Hoop. Shaughnessy studied fine art at Miami University in Ohio (B.F.A.) and the School of the Art Institute of Chicago (M.F.A.). Her work has been published in a new book called *The New Crewel* (Lark Books, 2005). An online portfolio is available at www.katherineshaughnessy.com.

JEN SWEARINGTON is the creator of Jennythreads, hand-dyed silk clothing and accessories. Her contemporary, mixed-media quilts are exhibited nationally, and she is an adjunct professor at the University of North Carolina at Asheville. Check out her work at www.jennythreads.net.

TERRY TAYLOR is a versatile project coordinator and editor at Lark Books. He is a prolific designer and exhibiting artist, working in media from metals and jewelry to paper crafts and mosaics. Terry has written several Lark Books, including *Altered Art* (2004), *Artful Eggs* (2004), and *The Weekend Crafter: Paper Crafting* (2002). He is coauthor of Lark's well-received children's series: *The Book of Wizard Crafts* (2001); *The Book of Wizard Parties* (2002); and *Wizard Magic* (2003). At last count, Terry's project designs have been published in more than 60 Lark books.

Index